CAMPAIGN • 209

NIAGARA 1814

The final invasion

JON LATIMER

ILLUSTRATED BY GRAHAM TURNER

Series editors Marcus Cowper and Nikolai Bogdanovic

First published in Great Britain in 2009 by Osprey Publishing,
Midland House, West Way, Botley, Oxford OX2 0PH, UK
443 Park Avenue South, New York, NY 10016, USA
E-mail: info@ospreypublishing.com

A CIP catalogue record for this book is available from the British Library.

ISBN: 978 1 84603 439 8

PDF e-book ISBN: 978 1 84603 887 7

Editorial by Ilios Publishing Ltd, Oxford, UK (www.iliospublishing.com)
Page layout by: The Black Spot
Index by Alan Thatcher
Typeset in Sabon and Myriad Pro
Maps by Bounford.com
3D bird's-eye views by The Black Spot
Battlescene illustrations by Graham Turner
Originated by PDQ Media
Printed in China through Worldprint

09 10 11 12 13   10 9 8 7 6 5 4 3 2 1

FOR A CATALOGUE OF ALL BOOKS PUBLISHED BY OSPREY MILITARY AND
AVIATION PLEASE CONTACT:

NORTH AMERICA
Osprey Direct, c/o Random House Distribution Center, 400 Hahn Road,
Westminster, MD 21157
E-mail: uscustomerservice@ospreypublishing.com

ALL OTHER REGIONS
Osprey Direct, The Book Service Ltd, Distribution Centre, Colchester Road,
Frating Green, Colchester, Essex, CO7 7DW
E-mail: customerservice@ospreypublishing.com

www.ospreypublishing.com

DEDICATION

To the memory of Jon Latimer, 24 June 1964–4 January 2009.

ARTIST'S NOTE

Readers may care to note that the original paintings from which the
color plates in this book were prepared are available for private sale.
All reproduction copyright whatsoever is retained by the Publishers.
All enquiries should be addressed to:

Graham Turner
PO Box 568
Aylesbury
Buckinghamshire
HP17 8ZK
UK

www.studio88.co.uk

The Publishers regret that they can enter into no correspondence
upon this matter.

THE WOODLAND TRUST

Osprey Publishing are supporting the Woodland Trust, the UK's leading
woodland conservation charity, by funding the dedication of trees.

Key to military symbols

CONTENTS

The northern theatre of war, 1814

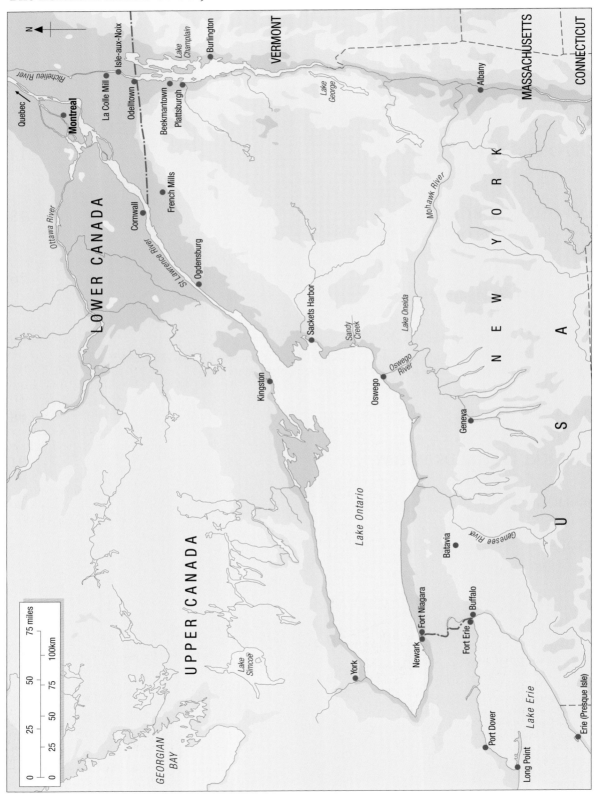

ORIGINS OF THE CAMPAIGN

By late 1813, despite some success in western Upper Canada (Ontario), the tide of war in North America was beginning to turn against the United States. As the year drew to a close Britain and her Continental allies anticipated securing final victory over France and, with the Royal Navy's blockade of the eastern seaboard seriously undermining the American economy, American prospects in her war with Britain appeared bleak, as British forces in Canada could also now expect large reinforcements of veteran troops.

Despite defeat on Lake Erie and the Thames River in 1813, the British retained control in the far west of the vast area around Lake Michigan, thanks to possession of the tiny posts of Michilimackinac and Prairie du Chien. This ensured the continuing support of Chippawa, Ottawa, Menominee, Winnebago, Fox, Sac and Sioux Indians, and enabled a very small number of British troops to control an area far greater than that of Britain itself. The American Secretary of War, John Armstrong, reasoned that the British would want to re-establish themselves on the Thames and he wished to frustrate any such plans. But if the

John Bull making a new batch of ships to send to the lakes. A satire on British naval defeats on the Great Lakes in 1813. King George III feeds a tray of small ships into a bread oven and says: 'Ay! What … Brother Jonathan taken another whole fleet on the Lakes – Must work away – Work away & send some more or He'll have Canada next.' (Toronto Public Library, T-14654)

The attack on Fort Niagara. To approach Fort Niagara the British forlorn hope stormed two taverns containing American soldiers, and succeeded in preventing the alarm being raised. When the guard then marched out to relieve those on duty they rushed the gate and secured entry. (Drawing by George Balbar, courtesy of Haunted Press)

United States was to have any success in the peace negotiations due to take place at Ghent in the Netherlands, she needed to achieve a significant and tangible battlefield success while she still had the chance.

The previous autumn's campaign against Montreal had been a severe setback for the United States; not only had the attempt by Major-General James Wilkinson ended in ignominious failure, but gains made earlier in the year in the Niagara Peninsula had been steadily eroded. The garrison of Fort George on the Canadian shore under the command of Brigadier-General of New York militia George McClure comprised just a handful of regulars, some 250 pro-American Indians, and about 1,000 militiamen badly affected by a perennial problem besetting US forces: arrears of pay.

A temporary respite came for McClure in November when Major-General William Henry Harrison arrived at Buffalo with some 1,200 westerners, following his successful campaign along the Thames River; but he soon departed and McClure's position rapidly deteriorated. Despite offering illegal bounties to his militiamen they drifted away, and when their terms of enlistment expired they were discharged without pay. Left with just 60 regulars he made plans to evacuate the fort and burn it down when, on 10 December, he heard a rumour that the British were 'advancing in force' and hurriedly abandoned the post, but only after burning the 150 private homes of Newark and turning out the inhabitants in zero-degree weather, leaving the once beautiful town turned to 'ruin, nothing to be seen but brick chimneys standing'.

On 16 December a new British commander, Lieutenant-General Sir Gordon Drummond, arrived in the Niagara Peninsula as military commander and administrator of Upper Canada. Drummond had orders to exploit any American weakness, and was furious at the destruction of Newark. Preparations to attack Fort Niagara on the US shore began immediately, although the Americans had taken the precaution of destroying river craft

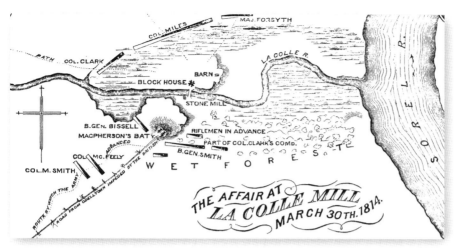

La Colle Mill, 30 March 1814. La Colle Mill (modern Cantic, Quebec) was a stone fortification on the river of the same name, defended by 180 men including 70 Royal Marines under Major Richard Butler Handcock of the 13th (Somerset) Regiment. (Benson J. Lossing, *Pictorial Field Book of the War of 1812*, New York, 1868)

and only two boats could be located. Nevertheless Canadian militia eagerly volunteered to fetch sufficient *bateaux* – shallow draught transports – from Burlington 80km away, carried down by night across the snow and carefully concealed in Longhurst Ravine out of sight of the American shore.

On 18 December 562 men – 12 Royal Artillerymen, the Grenadier Company of 1st Battalion, 1st Regiment (The Royal Scots), the flank companies of the 41st, whose two battalions had been consolidated following the disaster of the Thames, and 350 men of the 100th Regiment (The Prince Regent's County of Dublin Regiment) – under the command of Lieutenant-Colonel John Murray, assembled at St David's and carefully approached the Niagara River via ground hiding them from American eyes. At 10pm on a bitterly cold night they set off across the water. All knew it was an extremely risky operation, to be carried out by the bayonet with unloaded muskets.

The forlorn hope stormed a tavern containing American soldiers and a second public house on the way to Youngstown was similarly dealt with. Reaching the fort they found the drawbridge down, and rushed the gate. The British then split into three groups but made the mistake of cheering which roused the defenders, who began firing from the interiors of the buildings. Their women, 'supposing we had Indians with us, were greatly frightened', recalled Private George Ferguson of the 100th Regiment, 'and ran around shrieking most piteously'. The defenders had taken no precautions and McClure reported with horror: 'Our men were nearly all asleep in their tents, the Enemy rushed in and commenced a most horrid slaughter.' The British inflicted 65 dead and 14 wounded, mostly with the bayonet, and took 350 prisoners including the commander, Captain Nathaniel Leonard, who was at home five kilometres away and rode up to the gate and into the bag; the attackers suffered only five wounded and six killed in return.

Soon afterwards McClure was replaced in command by Major-General Amos Hall who was able to cover the retreat, as over the next couple of weeks the British laid waste to Black Rock, Lewiston and Buffalo. 'The whole frontier from Lake Ontario to Lake Erie is depopulated', lamented New York's Governor, Daniel D. Tompkins, '& the buildings & improvements, with a few exceptions, destroyed.' It was a significant coup for the British who would hold Fort Niagara until the end of hostilities, and in barely one month Drummond had more than cancelled the American successes of the previous summer and brought 'hard war' to American soil.

The Capture of Fort Niagara commissioned by 52nd (Niagara) Battery, Royal Artillery. This painting by Dawn Waring shows Lieutenant George Charlton RA and his detachment of gunners. The buildings are not exactly as they were at the time, the ration store on the right having been built since. (Friends of Old Fort Niagara)

For the year's forthcoming campaign practically every American agreed that the British naval base at Kingston had to be the primary objective, but Armstrong would instead end up directing operations against Niagara, in part because of continuing communications problems with his commanders in the field. First Wilkinson decided to break up his camp at French Mills to which he had retreated at the end of 1813, and at the end of January ordered Brigadier-General Jacob Brown to march 2,000 men of his Northern Army to Sackets Harbor, while he took the rest to Plattsburgh.

They prepared to move on 3 February, burning the flotilla including 12 gunboats and dozens of river craft stuck in the St Lawrence ice, their blockhouses and accommodation and any stores they could not carry away. The sick, still numbering over 400, were sent by sleigh to Burlington, and the army marched out on the 9th. Spies reported this activity to the British at Cornwall and Lieutenant-Colonel Joseph Morrison of the 2nd/89th Regiment decided to take pre-emptive action, and sent a raid on Madrid, New York, where a sale of goods taken during the invasion was being organized. The Americans were then pursued by a small detachment of the 89th and 103rd regiments close to Plattsburgh, which took 100 sleigh-loads of stores including one carrying a hogshead of whiskey, although the contents never reached Canada as 'soldiers ran up behind the sleigh, bored a hole with a bayonet, and secured in jugs the coveted fluid'.

The British were now free to roam the south bank of the St Lawrence at will creating a great feeling of insecurity among the inhabitants, although around 91 soldiers took the opportunity to desert and Prevost complained of the standard of soldier sent out to him; too many were convicts from the hulks and no manner of discipline would turn them into soldiers. Meanwhile throughout January and February Armstrong prepared to relieve the hapless Wilkinson of

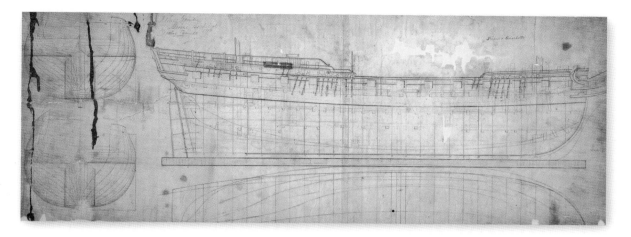

his command, but was not ready to make a decision until 24 March. He was too late; with his keen nose for trouble Wilkinson decided to lead another foray into British territory, marching 4,000 men towards Montreal while requesting a court martial to clear him of the 'slanders and misrepresentations' he was suffering from the press over the previous year's campaign.

On 30 March American light troops entered Odelltown followed by three infantry brigades accompanied by a squadron of light dragoons and 11 guns, and drove off the British pickets. They then attacked the post at Burton Ville held by two Canadian companies, who gave them such a warm reception that they were turned aside to attack the nearby post at Lacolle Mill (modern Cantic, Quebec), a stone fortification on the river of the same name, defended by 180 men including 70 Royal Marines under Major Richard Butler Handcock of the 13th (Somerset) Regiment. (It seems probable that the designation of the 13th as light infantry in 1822 came as a result of their service in North America where they were commanded by Lieutenant-Colonel William Williams, formerly of the 60th Regiment, who trained them extensively in light infantry tactics as being appropriate to the forests of the country.)

Now, having cleared a wood before the post and cut off Handcock's line of retreat, Wilkinson laboriously brought up two 12-pdr guns to assault the position, but they made little impression on the structure, despite having an 18-pdr available nearby. Soon afterwards the flank companies of the 13th Regiment arrived from the blockhouse at Isle-aux-Noix, and Handcock ordered them to cross the river and charge the guns, which they did but were driven off. Further reinforcements then arrived in the form of the Grenadier Company of the Canadian Fencibles and a company of Voltigeurs Canadien who from snow melt 'were obliged to wade through mud and water up to their waists for many miles'. These four companies renewed the assault and drove the American gunners from their pieces, although they were unable to hold the position.

The British were then further reinforced by two gunboats coming down the Richelieu River and the Americans were forced to retire. British losses were 13 killed and 50 wounded to 144 Americans killed, wounded and missing. Wilkinson gave up and retired to the United States having finally had enough; but his court of inquiry did not sit until January 1815 and on 21 March he was acquitted of all charges, although Congress had by then reduced the Army and he was dropped from the rolls, his long and ignominious career finally ended.

Plans of HMS *Princess Charlotte*. Built at the Kingston Royal Naval Dockyard exclusively for service on Lake Ontario, HMS *Princess Charlotte* was originally laid down as a transport brig named *Vittoria*. She carried 24 long 24-pdrs and 16 32-pdr carronades and was launched on 15 April 1814. (Library and Archives Canada, NMC-97256)

Meanwhile north of the border the British Government provided a much needed £100,000 in specie to relieve the financial pressure in Canada, and in April Drummond proposed that with 4,000 men he could destroy Sackets Harbor, the main US naval base on Lake Ontario, for which purpose he needed only 800–1,000 reinforcements from Lower Canada. By early May he was in a position to launch a preliminary attack against Oswego where Lieutenant-Colonel George A. Mitchell of the 3rd US Artillery arrived on 30 April with a small detachment, to find its fort rotten with few guns, and started hurriedly repairing the defences.

Throughout the spring the rivalry between the two navies on Lake Ontario continued apace, with the balance in the crucial shipbuilding race finely poised, and although the launch of *Prince Regent* (56 guns) and *Princess Charlotte* (42) on 14 April gave the British an advantage of about 25 guns overall, this was still not enough to change the Royal Navy's cautious stance into an aggressive one. Rumours arriving from the American shore also prompted the laying down of a third frigate that would eventually grow into a behemoth of oceanic proportions more powerful than Nelson's flagship at Trafalgar – HMS *St Lawrence* (102). On 1 May the US Navy launched *Superior* (64) – built in just 80 days – but with the American shipbuilding programme not due for completion before July the British had temporary control of the lake. Drummond's force of 900 troops sailed from Kingston on 4 May and arrived at Oswego the following morning to find the Americans in no position to make an effective defence, but adverse winds drove the attackers off.

Next morning conditions improved and through waist-deep water Lieutenant-Colonel Victor Fischer led ashore six companies of Régiment de Watteville, one of Glengarry Light Infantry and one from 2nd Battalion, Royal Marines, with supporting detachments of gunners and sappers, and a party of sailors under Captain William Mulcaster RN. Since almost all the troops landed in deep water their ammunition was rendered useless, so they fixed bayonets and advanced under heavy fire. While the company of Glengarry Light Infantry cleared the woods to the left, the main body and the sailors advanced on the village and made a frontal attack against the fort. The Americans drawn up on the glacis fell back and as the attackers reached the top of the slope, the defenders abandoned the fort and fled. The Americans lost six men killed, 38 wounded and 25 missing. The British lost 18 killed and 73 wounded, including the valuable Mulcaster who was seriously wounded by grapeshot, losing a leg. The British destroyed the barracks and stores and carried away 2,400 barrels of pork, salt and flour, and seven heavy guns, although most of the heavy ordnance had already been shifted to Oswego Falls 19km away, so the attack was only a partial success.

Then at the end of the month came disaster for the British; on 28 May the US naval commander, Commodore Isaac Chauncey, was moving stores by boat up to Sackets Harbor using 130 men of 1st US Rifle Regiment under Major Daniel Appling, and a similar number of pro-American Indians as escort moving along the shore. The following day Captain Stephen Popham RN, leading 200 seamen and Royal Marines, attacked the Americans in boats; but when Popham landed near Sandy Creek the British were ambushed by a detachment of riflemen. They lost 19 killed and 28 wounded, and a further 133 sailors and Marines, two Royal Navy captains and four lieutenants, and two Royal Marine lieutenants captured, for the loss of one rifleman and one Indian killed. It was a humiliating defeat that was all the more costly because the British absolutely could not afford to lose seamen.

However, despite this success the worsening strategic situation in early 1814 meant that the American authorities could do little more than trust regional commanders and hope for the best, while the British could be expected to apply pressure on all frontiers and coasts. Time was rapidly running out for the United States to make effective gains; they had to achieve local superiority somewhere, and as the bulk of British forces were deployed around Montreal the cabinet favoured the western theatre. It therefore seems the Niagara campaign was something of an afterthought to Armstrong's desire to help his friends in the west, by giving troops who would otherwise be unoccupied something to do.

CHRONOLOGY

1813

10 December	US forces destroy Newark
16 December	Lt. Gen. Drummond arrives to command British forces in Upper Canada
18 December	British capture Fort Niagara
30 December	British forces destroy Buffalo

1814

24 March	US Secretary of War John Armstrong decides to replace Maj. Gen. James Wilkinson
30 March	Battle of La Colle Mill
14 April	The Royal Navy launches *Prince Regent* and *Princess Charlotte* on Lake Ontario
30 April	Armstrong submits plan for Niagara campaign to US cabinet
1 May	US Navy launches *Superior* on Lake Ontario
6 May	British raid and capture Oswego
9 May	British reinforcements for North America begin to leave Europe
28 May	Battle of Sandy Creek
6 June	Maj. Gen. Brown assumes command of the Left Division
11 June	US Navy launches *Mohawk* on Lake Ontario
3 July	US forces cross over to the Niagara Peninsula and capture Fort Erie

5 July	Battle of Chippawa
18 July	US forces destroy St David's
20 July	The Ancaster 'Bloody Assizes' end with executions
25 July	Battle of Lundy's Lane
3 August	Battle of Conjocta Creek and British invest Fort Erie
5 August	Brig. Gen. Edmund P. Gaines assumes command of Fort Erie
10 August	US Navy launches *Eagle* on Lake Champlain
13 August	British siege artillery commences its bombardment of Fort Erie
15 August	British Assault on Fort Erie
25 August	The Royal Navy launches *Confiance* on Lake Champlain
29 August	Second British siege battery commences bombardment of Fort Erie
1 September	British forces cross the New York state border west of Lake Champlain
10 September	The Royal Navy launches *St Lawrence* on Lake Ontario
11 September	Battle of Plattsburgh
17 September	US sortie from Fort Erie
19 October	Battle of Cook's Mills
5 November	Americans destroy and abandon Fort Erie and the campaign ends

OPPOSING COMMANDERS

Major-General Jacob Jennings Brown, US Army (1775–1822). Originally opposed to the war, Jacob Brown nevertheless fought more pitched battles more successfully than any other American general, yet he is largely forgotten today. But his calm, practical and orderly character made him ideally suited for high command. (Library and Archives Canada, C-100390)

AMERICAN COMMANDERS

Following Wilkinson's failures a significant change in the US Army's command arrangements was finally instigated. After the fiasco at Châteauguay in November, Brigadier-General Wade Hampton had been quietly invalided out by Armstrong who, in December 1813, recommended promoting George Izard and Thomas Flournoy to major-general while passing over the promising Andrew Jackson and Jacob Brown. Despite mounting pressure to remove his Secretary of War, President James Madison continued to support Armstrong, but he nominated Izard and Brown to Congress instead. Soon enterprising young colonels including Alexander Macomb, Edmund P. Gaines, Winfield Scott and Eleazar W. Ripley, with an average age of 33, were promoted to brigadier-general. However, William Henry Harrison resigned in May when it became apparent that he was being sidelined.

With promotion **Jacob Brown** was to command the Left Division of Military District No. 9, or 'the Army of the North', extending into Vermont where Izard, at Plattsburgh, commanded the Right Division. Brown's command was also sometimes referred to as the 1st Division, or the Army of the Niagara. Brown was a man underestimated by many. Born of Quaker origins in Bucks County, Pennsylvania, Brown graduated from the University of Pennsylvania in 1790 and became a teacher, moving to upstate New York in 1798. He became known as 'Smuggler', or 'Potash' Brown, after his part in the so-called 'Potash Rebellion' of 1807. When the war began, he was a brigadier-general of New York militia, and soon demonstrated his abilities as more senior officers floundered. Resourceful and open to new ideas, he was also very determined, although this could turn to obstinacy. Having little patience with military pomp and circumstance he was able to get more out of his citizen soldiers than most other officers, but despite being one of the few commanders to distinguish himself the previous autumn his background as a militia general meant his promotion was nevertheless a gamble; both Wilkinson and Winfield Scott regarded him contemptuously as an amateur, although he was nothing of the sort.

The 28-year-old Virginian **Winfield Scott** was a long service regular who would eventually become general-in-chief of the US Army by the time of the Civil War, but for now he commanded a brigade under Brown. At 1.95m tall broad shouldered and stern featured, he was among the most experienced officers in the army. Scott was born on his family's plantation near Petersburg, Virginia, and educated at the College of William & Mary. He was first a lawyer

and a Virginia militia cavalry corporal before being commissioned a captain in the artillery in 1808, then serving in Louisiana where he fell foul of Wilkinson resulting in a year's suspension of duty, which was no disgrace.

A natural and aggressive leader, Scott was also impetuous to the point of rashness, and suffered from vanity born of intense ambition. But the other brigades were also now commanded by competent men of experience; the second brigade would come under the command of 32-year-old **Eleazar W. Ripley** who was, in contrast to Scott, a cool and reserved character who did not inspire the same personal loyalty. A Massachusetts native and Dartmouth College graduate, as a lawyer and politician Ripley's support for the war went against the general sentiment in New England, but earned him command of the 21st Infantry, which he turned into an efficient unit. His political instincts ensured he made the public aware of this, which helped gain him promotion in April 1814 but which angered fellow officers. An ADC commented that though brave, he was 'too much of a Yankee [too cold] for me'.

The third or militia brigade came under the command of **Peter B. Porter**, who succeeded Amos Hall when the latter resigned in disgust at the failure to secure arms or pay for his men. A resident of Black Rock and successful partner in the Porter, Barton Company with key business interests in expansionist road projects in the Niagara region, Porter was a pre-war politician who became Chairman of the Foreign Affairs Committee in 1811, and together with other 'War Hawks' pushed President Madison for a breach with Britain. Unlike most politicians, however, he was prepared to back his words with action, and served conscientiously throughout the war. Porter's business and political connections and easy-going manner earned him numerous friends, and, furthermore, he was confident the New York militia could be persuaded to cross the frontier where it had previously proved reluctant to serve.

BRITISH COMMANDERS

As Governor-in-Chief of British North America, **Lieutenant-General Sir George Prevost** had proved an able administrator, and as military commander had successfully held the line against repeated American invasion attempts, juggling his limited resources with skill. His senior commanders in the field, however, were less experienced. Born in Quebec in 1772, **Gordon Drummond** was the third son of Colin Drummond, laird of Megginch in Perthshire and deputy paymaster general of British forces in Canada. Drummond would therefore

LEFT
Red Jacket, Seneca War Chief (c.1750–1830). Red Jacket took his name – one of several – from a favourite embroidered coat given to him by the British for wartime services during the American Revolution. His other name, Sagoyewatha ('He Keeps Them Awake'), came from his oratory ability. (Archives of Ontario)

RIGHT
Lieutenant-General Gordon Drummond, British Army (1772–1854). In 1816 Drummond returned to Britain and was honoured for his contribution to the American War. He received a knighthood and a promotion to full general, although his post-war career was unremarkable. (*General Sir Gordon Drummond* by George Theodore Berthon, c.1882, Government of Ontario Art Collection, Archives of Ontario)

Major-General Phineas Riall, British Army (1775–1850). Being wounded and captured at Lundy's Lane marked the end of Riall's active career, but in 1816 he was appointed Lieutenant Governor of Grenada, a post he held until 1823. Thereafter, he appears to have seen very little service, and he died peacefully in Paris in 1850. (Riall Family)

become the first Canadian-born officer to command the government in 1815, taking over as Governor General and Administrator of Canada, although his post-war career was unremarkable.

Drummond had joined the 1st (Royal Scots) Regiment as an ensign in 1789 and within five years had risen by purchase to become lieutenant-colonel of the 8th (The King's) Regiment aged just 21. He commanded the regiment on active service in the Netherlands in the ill-fated expedition of 1795, then in the Mediterranean, Egypt in 1801 and the West Indies. He was promoted brigadier-general in 1804 and major-general the following year, serving as second in command at Jamaica and Canada. After serving in Canada as major-general between 1808 and 1811 he was promoted lieutenant-general with command of a military district in Ireland. Appointment to his first active command in Upper Canada was on the basis of his North American experience, but his stern features and outward composure did not inspire one local dignitary, the Reverend John Strachan, who thought he 'lacked the 'military fire and vigour of decision which the principal commander of this country must possess in order to preserve it'.

Drummond was accompanied by 38-year old Irishman **Major-General Phineas Riall** who would take over from the ailing Brigadier-General John Vincent in command of all troops west of Kingston, a command that now became the Right Division. Vincent temporarily took command of the troops at Kingston and along the St Lawrence, which became the Centre Division, and would in due course be replaced by Major-General Richard Stovin. Riall was the younger son of an Anglo-Irish banking family from Clonmel, County Tipperary, and had entered the army in March 1794 aged 18. By December he was a major in the 128th Regiment, but went on half pay in 1798 when the unit disbanded. He first saw active service that year during the Irish 'troubles' but most of his experience came as a major in the 15th (Yorkshire East Riding) Regiment in the West Indies in 1803. He briefly commanded a brigade during 1809–10 in the attacks on Martinique, the Saintes and Guadeloupe, was promoted colonel on his return to Britain in 1810, and made major-general two years later. He was described by Captain William H. Merritt of the locally raised Niagara Light Horse as 'very brave, near sighted, rather short, but stout', and to be 'thought by some rather rash'.

They were supported on the lake by the Royal Navy squadron of **Commodore Sir James Lucas Yeo RN**, who succeeded better than Chauncey in supporting his army. Crucially the American cabinet was under the impression that Chauncey's squadron would be available to support Brown, and Armstrong would lead Brown to believe he would be available to do so no later than 15 July; but Chauncey was fixated with engaging Yeo's squadron on the lake and had no intention of being deflected from this task in order to assist the Army.

OPPOSING FORCES

AMERICAN FORCES

Although the advance across the Niagara was to be the American main effort for the region in 1814, Brown had fewer than 3,400 effectives in the Left Division. The 2,400 regulars were mostly New Englanders who volunteered for regular service in large numbers despite the general lack of enthusiasm for the war in that section. They would be organized in two brigades and supported by an artillery battalion of 300 serving as infantry, together with 480 Pennsylvania volunteers under Porter who found that few New York militia were prepared to cross the frontier after all, but who suggested that Indian warriors be engaged to participate instead. He then persuaded the Seneca chief Red Jacket to provide some 500 warriors from the Iroquois of the Six Nations, thus paving the way for civil war with their Grand River brethren to the west serving with the British.

On 20 April Brown and Scott were in the process of laying out a camp near Buffalo when Brown received a panicky communication from Brigadier-General Edmund P. Gaines, commanding at Sackets Harbor. Brown decided to investigate and turned over command to Scott with orders to pay close attention to the state of the infantry. Scott then began intensively training his

Winfield Scott training the Left Division. Scott's 'camp of instruction' soon took on almost legendary significance, promoted not least by Scott himself. The uniforms shown in this woodcut from an early biography of the 1840s are, however, inaccurate. (From D. H. Strother, *Illustrated Life of General Winfield Scott*, New York 1847)

brigade at a 'camp of instruction', something since mythologized, not least by Scott himself (how the young brigadier, through discipline and drill, turned ragtag recruits into soldiers capable of defeating the British on the open field). But it was not basic training for raw recruits, as many writers have assumed, rather advanced battle training for already seasoned soldiers.

Scott was pleased to see that the four regiments under his command – the 9th, 11th, 21st and 25th US infantry – were experienced, having served in the abortive campaign against Montreal the previous autumn, and he well knew their 'high Character for discipline – patience under fatigues and conduct in view of danger'. He boasted to a friend that if, 'of such materials, I do not make the best army now in service by the 1st June, I will agree to be dismissed [from] the service'. The tall figure of Scott gave the men of the Left Division intensive instruction at Flint Hill between April and June 1814, and his relentless attention to detail would pay off handsomely during the campaign.

He also rapidly improved the administration and hygiene of the force, dramatically reducing the sick list, and attended to their equipment, although he could not find enough blue uniforms for his men; they had been shipped in plenty of time for once but had been diverted to Plattsburgh and Sackets Harbor, and only enough were found from one source or another to clothe the 21st Infantry. Eventually Commissary-General Callender Irvine had to have 2,000 uniforms hastily run up and sent to Buffalo, but there being insufficient blue cloth, short grey jackets were substituted instead.

Fort Erie in more peaceful times. Drawn just a year before the war, this view of Fort Erie was made from Buffalo Creek on the American shore by Edward Walsh of the 49th (Hertfordshire) Regiment. The whole area in the foreground was long ago consumed by the city of Buffalo. (Library and Archives Canada, C-17551)

One problem Scott struggled with was the lack of a standard drill manual in the US Army, and he adopted the French system originally modified by Brigadier-General Alexander Smyth in 1812. He then set about drilling his men relentlessly, for seven to ten hours every day with frequent inspections, blank firing exercises and mock battles, first by companies, then by regiments. He then began to manoeuvre the regiments together, much to the delight of the soldiers 'who began to perceive why they had been made to fag so long', related Drummer Jarvis Hanks of the 11th US Infantry, so that the effort 'made us well acquainted with our business as soldiers and fit us for the contests which were expected during the summer in the enemy's camp'. Certainly it would prove to be a significant development, and while most of the Pennsylvanians assigned to the operation, like the New York militia, were reluctant to cross the border, Corporal John Witherow was among those who did and was extremely impressed by the training the regulars were performing under Scott. By mid-May enough reinforcements had arrived to enable Brown to form a second regular brigade under Ripley, yet all the units involved were seriously below establishment strength, at around barely 40 per cent. And so, although highly potent, Brown's Army was also very fragile.

BRITISH FORCES

The forces they would be going up against in defence of Canada were based on the regular British Army, which had proved comfortably superior in quality to the raw troops the Americans could deploy in the early years of the war. In early 1814 their numbers remained small, but they were long-term

regulars and ably supported by the Canadian militia, drawn from the entire population but organized to provide field units from among the most dedicated and active citizens, while the remainder provided essential logistical support. Determined to defend their homes and commanded by regular officers, they proved more effective than their American counterparts, whose officer ranks were taken as being equivalent to those of US regulars however inexperienced the holder.

Late in April the British Government sought to reinforce Prevost following the defeat of the French in the peninsula, and on 9 May the first units – 4th Battalion, 1st Regiment (The Royal Scots), and the 97th (Queen's Own Germans) Regiment – left Portsmouth and Cork respectively. On 3 June the Government sent an outline that substantial reinforcements were on the way, although Prevost did not receive this letter until the second week of July. The 4th Royal Scots would be joined at Quebec by the Nova Scotia Fencibles from Newfoundland, the 90th (Perthshire Volunteers) Regiment from the West Indies and 1st/6th (1st Warwickshire) and 1st/82nd (Prince of Wales' Volunteers) regiments from Bordeaux, to be followed by 'twelve of the most effective Regiments' from Wellington's army, plus three Royal Artillery companies – some 13,000 men in total, while other forces would harass the American coast.

Until they arrived, however, the defence of the Niagara Peninsula rested on the 2,500 British troops stationed there or nearby, comprising units such as 1st Royal Scots, 1st/8th, 41st, 2nd/89th and 104th (New Brunswick) regiments, most of whom now had widespread experience of operating and fighting in the country, and others less seasoned including the 103rd Regiment. They could also count on Canadian units trained and equipped as regulars, such as the Glengarry Light Infantry and the Incorporated Militia

LEFT

41st Regiment of Foot. Having served in Canada since 1799, a second battalion of the 41st Regiment was raised in August 1812, and in 1813 the two battalions were consolidated. The uniforms shown are the 1st Battalion (left) and 2nd Battalion (right), which the regiment would have been wearing in 1814. (Courtesy of Eric Manders, from *Military Uniforms in America. Years of Growth, 1796–1851* © The Company of Military Historians, 1977)

RIGHT

100th Regiment of Foot (The Prince Regent's County of Dublin Regiment). The 100th was raised in 1804, mainly from Northern Ireland, and transferred to Nova Scotia in 1805. In 1816 the regiment was renumbered the 99th, then disbanded at Chatham in 1818. (From *Military Uniforms in America. Years of Growth, 1796–1851* © The Company of Military Historians, 1977)

Battalion of Upper Canada, and they were generally well supported by the Royal Navy on Lake Ontario – in contrast to America's muddled approach to service cooperation. Thus British preparations, however imperfect, were generally successful thanks to a measure of understanding between army and navy. However, the strategic consequences of defeat at Sandy Creek were felt immediately as Yeo was forced to release his blockade on Sackets Harbor and Oswego, enabling the Americans to complete the ships needed to contest control of the lake.

In early June Yeo reported that he was already short of 280 seamen and that when HMS *St Lawrence* was ready he would need 680 more. On 11 June Chauncey launched *Mohawk* (42) making the total number of vessels about equal but giving 251 American guns to 222 British; the Americans also had a manpower superiority of some 3,300 to 1,500 men. And this precarious balance would profoundly affect what transpired on land, because Chauncey remained determined to confront the British naval squadron rather than to support the army. The perennial problem with this strategy, however, was that the respective strengths of the two squadrons – in short-range carronades versus long guns – meant that whenever they met they both manoeuvred to gain maximum advantage, yet what was advantageous to one was inimical to the other, and as a result no decisive action was ever fought.

ORDERS OF BATTLE

AMERICAN FORCES

CHIPPAWA, 5 JULY

General Officer Commanding, Left Division – Maj. Gen. Jacob Brown

1st Brigade – Brig. Gen. Winfield Scott

    9th/22nd US Infantry (549) – Maj. Henry Leavenworth

    11th US Infantry (416) – Maj. John McNeil

    25th US Infantry (354) – Maj. Thomas Jesup

    Coy, 21st US Infantry (~ 80) – Capt. Benjamin Ropes

3rd (Militia) Brigade – Brig. Gen. Peter B. Porter

    5th Pennsylvania Militia (Fenton's) (540) – Maj. James Woods

    Canadian Volunteers (56) – Lt. Col. Joseph Willcocks

    Six Nations warriors (386) – Lt. Col. Erastus Granger

US Artillery (two x 6-pdrs, three x 12-pdrs, one x 5½in. howitzer) – Maj. Jacob Hindman

Detachment, US Light Dragoons (70) – Capt. Samuel D. Harris

LUNDY'S LANE, 25 JULY

General Officer Commanding, Left Division – Maj. Gen. Jacob Brown

1st Brigade – Brig. Gen. Winfield Scott

    9th US Infantry (200) – Maj. Henry Leavenworth

    11th US Infantry (200) – Maj. John McNeil

    22nd US Infantry (300) – Col. Hugh Brady

    25th US Infantry (380) – Maj. Thomas Jesup

2nd Brigade – Brig. Gen. Eleazar W. Ripley

    1st US Infantry (150) – Lt. Col. Robert C. Nicholas

    21st US Infantry (432) – Col. James Miller (Included coy of 17th and two coys of 19th US infantry)

National colour of the 9th US Regiment of Infantry. Under the Act of 11 January 1812, the 9th Infantry was organized in March, being raised in New Hampshire and Massachusetts. But although part of the regular army, with a 'national' colour shown here, it was accredited to the latter state. (United States Military Academy, West Point)

BRITISH PLANS

Although the British already had some useful territorial bargaining counters, the Government in London was focused more clearly on the negotiating table than on military and naval realities in North America when it urged Prevost to press the war with all possible vigour, and to undertake offensive operations as soon as reinforcements arrived. The primary objective remained the security of Canada but Prevost should also consider the 'ultimate security' of British possessions in North America, necessitating offensive operations with a view to the complete destruction of Sackets Harbor and the American naval establishments on lakes Erie and Champlain. Prevost was also to retain Fort Niagara and look to retake Detroit and Michigan for the material benefit of the Indians.

However, these expectations were somewhat unreasonable, and in reply the ever-cautious Prevost wrote that as soon as all the promised troops arrived

Regimental colour of the 9th US Regiment of Infantry. The 9th Infantry was commanded by Major Henry Leavenworth, regarded as 'the ablest battalion officer in the army'. Attached to them in 1814 was a 200-man contingent of the 22nd US Infantry, recruited in New Jersey, Delaware and Pennsylvania. (United States Military Academy, West Point)

he would implement his instructions; but there were as yet no resources spare to attempt to regain Lake Erie without which there appeared little prospect of winning control of Michigan, and that in the meantime and until complete naval control of Lakes Ontario and Champlain was gained, he would have to confine himself to defensive operations. In order to hold an ace at the peace negotiations Prevost therefore decided the Champlain region offered the best prospects for an offensive, but no move in this direction could be anticipated before September. And while the Americans appeared weak on land, control of Lake Champlain would be essential so Prevost hoped that HMS *Confiance* (36) being built at Isle-aux-Noix would permit this once she was ready. Elsewhere his natural caution ensured that Drummond would have to defend the Niagara with the meagre resources already allotted to him, and this left the initiative in the hands of the Americans. But the question remained what would they choose to do with it.

THE NIAGARA CAMPAIGN

INVASION

By the early summer Scott's training programme was progressing well, although Brown's overall numbers remained small; however, the addition of Porter's militia brigade was not universally welcomed. Porter had hoped to be ready by 1 May but delays in receiving weapons and equipment saw this drift to mid-June, and Scott expressed a fear that 'we shall be disgraced if we admit a militia force either into our camp or order of battle'. Nevertheless, when Brown arrived on 6 June he was very pleased with his 'handsome little army'. Although Scott had not trained all the regulars – the 17th, 19th and 22nd US infantry did not arrive until the middle of the month, and the 23rd US Infantry marched in on 26 June – they took their lead from the standards he had set. But all the units remained under strength, and the militia particularly so, despite the addition of 56 Canadian volunteers, under the renegade former member of the Legislative Assembly for Upper Canada, Joseph Willcocks.

By July the Left Division was bored of constant drill and was spoiling for a fight. As one regular officer recalled 'every one was anxious of an opportunity to remove the disgrace which former disasters and defeats had attached to our arms, and to our military character'. When groups of Indians began to arrive in camp it was apparent that they would soon have their wish granted. Scott was visible everywhere and Surgeon William Horner remembered a visit to his hospital where he noted there was little work to do. 'No General', replied Horner, 'we are looking for some.' 'You will get it before long', said Scott. Finally, on the night of 2 July they received the order they had been waiting for; Brown informed the Left Division that it was to 'be put in motion against the enemy'.

By now the British troops scattered along the Niagara frontier were far less effective than those who seized Fort Niagara and raided Lewiston, Black Rock and Buffalo in January; the 1st/8th Regiment at Fort Niagara was plagued with sickness and desertion – actually increased when the men received an arrears of pay – and Riall was forced to replace them with the 100th Regiment. By the beginning of July there were 600 effectives of the 41st Regiment at Fort Niagara with 1,500 from 1st Royal Scots and the 100th Regiment garrisoning various posts along the shore, supported by a detachment of 19th Light Dragoons, two troops of Provincial Light Dragoons, the flank companies of the Lincoln militia and a dwindling company of militia artillery. A reserve of some 500 men of the 103rd Regiment was at Burlington and some 1,000 men of the Incorporated Militia Battalion of Upper Canada and the 1st/8th Regiment were now at York

The Niagara frontier

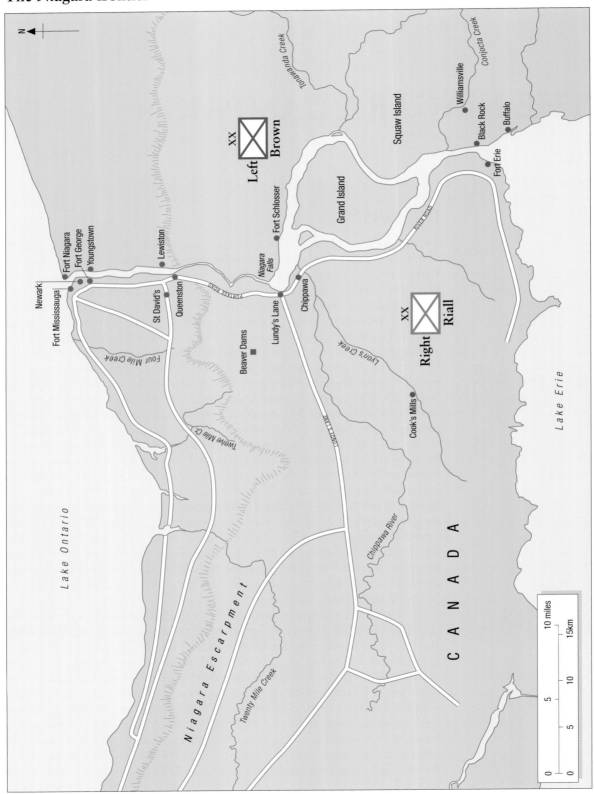

(modern Toronto), while the Glengarry Light Infantry and 2nd/89th Regiment were at Kingston. But the 25km stretch south of the Chippawa River could not be held or even patrolled effectively, and Riall was nervous of American moves in this area.

Early on the morning of 3 July the Americans were able to effect a landing quite easily at a point below Fort Erie. Originally built in 1764 on the Niagara River's edge, Fort Erie first saw action during the American Revolution, and a new fort was authorized in 1803 on the heights behind the original post, and constructed of formidable and readily available Onondaga flintstone. Major Thomas Buck of the 8th Regiment commanding the garrison with three guns and 137 men had been, according to his orders from Riall, set up 'to resist an attack short of an Invasion in force'. But when a large American force appeared he offered no serious resistance before surrendering. The formalities were concluded at 5pm, 'rather too soon perhaps to satisfy the claims of military etiquette', thought Porter, as the British marched out of the fort, and the stars and stripes were raised to the sound of Yankee Doodle on American fifes and drums. But at least the detachment of 19th Light Dragoons present had been able to set off to warn Riall of the enemy's approach.

The alarm sounded along the Canadian shore that Sunday was well remembered by Private George Ferguson of the 100th Regiment; a Methodist lay preacher, he had been given permission to leave Fort George and preach at a chapel between Queenston and Chippawa, where 'there came an express for a Militia officer who was in the congregation that the American army had crossed at Black Rock. This threw the congregation into confusion – the people ran to secure their effects – one running here and another there. I felt calm and tranquil, and my trust was in the Lord Jehovah.' Near the famous Falls some 300 Grand River Indian warriors under their half-Scottish, half-Cherokee war chief, John Norton, were camped as he prepared to reconnoitre the American shore; he received a summons from Lieutenant-Colonel Thomas Pearson commanding the flank companies of the 100th Regiment, who despite the abundant rumours reacted calmly and, joined by Norton's warriors, posted pickets before retiring to Chippawa that evening.

CHIPPAWA

On the morning of 4 July, Pearson advanced to Frenchman's Creek 13km south of Chippawa, now with the addition of the Light Company of 1st Royal Scots, a detachment of 19th Light Dragoons under Lieutenant William Horton and two brass 24-pdrs under Lieutenant Richard Armstrong RA. (These monsters had been cast as experimental pieces during the previous century and weighed 930kg without their carriages; they were the heaviest field pieces used by either side during the war.) Riall wanted to attack the Americans while they were preoccupied at Fort Erie, being still unaware of its fall, but he decided he was too weak to do so and chose to wait for the 1st/8th Regiment marching from York, who did not arrive until the following morning.

Scott's 1st Brigade was sent forward by Brown six kilometres to Frenchman's Creek, now covered by Pearson; his instructions were 'to secure a military position' or camp site but 'to be governed by circumstances'. The creek was flooded and the bridge planking was torn up, but the British retired, pausing at each subsequent creek for a dozen miles or so as the Americans set about repairing each crossing and following up. By the afternoon the Americans had

Lieutenant-Colonel Thomas Pearson, British Army (1781–1847). Thomas Pearson served extensively with the 23rd Regiment (Royal Welch Fusiliers) and was present at the battle of Albuera in 1811. Later that year he suffered a leg wound and returned to Britain on sick leave. Early in 1812, he went to Canada as Inspecting Field Officer of Militia. (Royal Welch Fusiliers Museum)

Major John McNeil, US Army (1784–1850). As a temporary regimental commander John McNeil's greatest difficulty proved not to be the enemy but his horse, which became uncontrollable with fear. But his cool leadership at Chippawa earned him brevet promotion to lieutenant-colonel. (Benson J. Lossing, *Pictorial Field Book of the War of 1812*, New York, 1868).

reached Street's (now Ussher's) Creek, two kilometres below Chippawa, and were greeted by the few now customary rounds from Armstrong's guns.

However, when Scott's left flank guard – Captain Turner Crooker's company of the 9th US Infantry – emerged upstream of the bridge, they saw the British guns apparently isolated, and forded the chest-deep water to reach an area of open ground to the north where they were in turn spotted by Horton's dragoons. Unsupported infantry was too much of a temptation for a good cavalryman, and Horton ordered an immediate charge across the open field as the Americans on the far bank watched in horror. However, Crooker kept his cool; his company fired a volley then retreated to take shelter in a farmhouse whence they kept up a steady fire, bringing down eight horses and wounding four dragoons, although the British guns escaped.

In the evening as it began to grow dark Scott saw the British assembled on the far bank of the Chippawa River, and with his men thirsty and tired he decided to retire three kilometres to make camp with his right flank resting on the Niagara River. There he was joined towards midnight by Brown with Ripley's Brigade and more artillery, and next morning by some Indians and the militia. Having marched some 24km in continuous rain, the Americans were cold and tired and lay down to rest, on ground that Captain Benjamin Ropes later recalled in atrocious spelling 'was covered with water owing to the Clayey surfise, this was the first rist that I had received from the Night of the First Inst. & it was very swift although wit & Lying as it was on water'.

During the night of 4/5 July Captain Joseph Henderson's picket of the 22nd US Infantry watched the strip of woods to the north of Street's Creek. In the morning, as the rain finally eased his company began to come under fire, and a desultory skirmishing continued all through the morning. With the arrival of the 1st/8th Regiment and the 1st and 2nd Lincoln regiments of militia, Riall now decided to attack, although he believed his 1,400 regulars, 200 militia – 2nd Lincolns were detailed to provide rear security – and 300 Indians were outnumbered two to one. The new commanding officer of the 100th Regiment was Lieutenant-Colonel George Hay, eighth marquess of Tweeddale, who had ridden into camp only to be struck down by fever. The 26-year-old twice-wounded Peninsula veteran was summoned to see Riall, but replied 'that I was in the cold fit of ague and I expected the hot fit in a short time'. Riall thoughtfully postponed the conference for an hour.

By midday, Brown was sick of the Canadian militia and Indians harassing his flank and, assuring Porter that there was not a 'single [regular] British soldier' south of the Chippawa, ordered him to 'scour the woods with [his] Indian force, sustained by the volunteers, and drive the enemy across' that river. In the afternoon of 5 July Porter's militia brigade was sent to drive off the British forces that had been raiding American pickets. Captain Samuel White recalled that having marched 29km 'without rations, it is not to be wondered at that not much alacrity was showed by the men to become of the party', and seemingly true to previous form his men broke and fled when they realized the entire British force was moving across the bridge towards them. The British deployed onto open ground bounded on their right by dense woods, and on their left by the Niagara River, but without the space to form a single line so that Riall ordered the 1st/8th Regiment to refuse the right flank.

As they advanced Private Ferguson recalled the rumour that the American front rank was composed of desperate men – 'deserters and Europeans'; another rumour ran that the Americans outnumbered the British five to one,

Militia and Indians fighting in the woods. The fight in the woods to the left flank of the American army was bitter and nasty. Both sides were so appalled that many Indians withdrew from the war as a result. (Drawing by George Balbar, courtesy of Haunted Press)

to which Riall supposedly replied: 'O, they are a set of cowardly untrained men – scape gallows or state prison men who will not stand the bayonet.' His hubristic confidence may have been born of prior experience against American troops, mainly militia, and he expected the Americans to wilt before resolute action in the same manner as on earlier occasions. But Hay already had his doubts about Riall after the general informed him that he intended to march straight down the river road and attack: when Hay pointed out the Americans would probably be in strength in the woods and attack the British on the march, Riall ignored him; this was exactly what happened, although fortunately Pearson's light infantry had already accounted for the threat, by driving the American Indians and militia back through the wood in a ferocious little action.

Riall soon discovered, however, that this American army was no disorganized rabble. Scott's Brigade, consisting of the combined 9th/22nd, 11th and 25th US infantry, which being dressed in grey Riall appears to have mistaken for militia, advanced to meet him on open ground, forsaking the relative security of its position behind a narrow creek in order to do so. As they came under artillery fire Drummer Jarvis Hanks recalled that the 'balls and grape, mostly passed over our heads and into the bend of the river', and Riall supposedly exclaimed in admiration at their steadiness: 'Why, these are regulars by God!' But Scott appears to be the only source for Riall's famous phrase, and there is no record of it in any British source.

Riall ordered 1st Royal Scots and the 100th Regiment to advance at about 4.30pm, directly at the American front. With the artillery of both sides engaged in a duel Scott now redirected the guns of Captain Nathan Towson, who was suffering from an eye infection at the time, to engage the advancing British

CHARGE OF HORTON'S DRAGOONS

Mounted cavalry actions were very rare during the American War. On 4 July at Street's Creek, a mile or so south of the Chippawa River, Captain Turner Crooker's **(1)** company **(2)** was able to ford the creek upstream of the bridge before the main body came up, only for Scott to watch in horror as they were charged by Lieutenant William Horton's **(3)** troop of 19th Light Dragoons **(4)**. The Americans reacted calmly, and fired a volley before withdrawing to a nearby farmhouse **(5)**. Originally raised as the 23rd Light Dragoons in 1781 for service in India where it arrived the following year, the regiment was renumbered the 19th four years later, and for 16 years it was the only British cavalry regiment in the subcontinent. After service in the Mahratta Wars and under Sir Arthur Wellesley at Assaye in 1802, the regiment finally embarked for England in 1806 where it remained until summoned to Canada in 1812. The vast nature of North America meant that the regiment served in scattered detachments, but by July 1814, its presence on the Niagara had been consolidated into two detachments of three officers and 71 men at Fort George, and three officers and 61 men at Long Point, while some 309 all-ranks served in the Plattsburgh expedition. In 1816 the regiment was redesignated as a lancer regiment but was disbanded in 1821. When the 19th Hussars were formed in 1862 from the 1st Bengal European Light Cavalry, they were granted permission to inherit the honours of the original 19th Light Dragoons.

infantry instead. Some 15 minutes later they approached to within about 60m when Scott ordered his men to fire, which the British returned, soon engulfing both lines in dense clouds of smoke. As the British infantry approached Scott noticed that the 8th Regiment was in a second line behind the 1st and 100th regiments that would enable him to outflank them to the west. But first a severe firefight ensued, in which both sides suffered greatly – a 'scene of carnage', recalled Lieutenant John Stevenson of the 100th Regiment. However, the British also had to endure American artillery firing canister while by now the British gunners were some way behind and unable to intervene effectively, and were forced to look on helplessly.

As Scott was busy on the plain, Brown prepared to support him with the remainder of the Left Division, in particular, on the western end of Scott's line. But before he could intervene the British found themselves disadvantaged by flanking fire from the 11th US Infantry under Major John McNeil. Born in New Hampshire, the enterprising McNeil had joined the army as a captain in 1812, and was 31 years old in 1814 when he assumed command of the 11th US Infantry early on the afternoon of 5 July after Colonel Thomas B. Campbell was wounded in the opening moments at Chippawa.

Meanwhile the 25th US Infantry under Major Thomas S. Jesup first drove back three companies of British light infantry near the woods – after coming 'within *grinning* distance', recalled Captain George Howard. The 25th then became engaged with the 1st/8th Regiment, and by attacking the

Trooper, 19th Light Dragoons. In late 1811 the Prince Regent chose a new light dragoon uniform very much resembling French *chasseurs à cheval*. Officers were dismayed, one noting in February 1812 that when 'Lord Guernsey showed us the new Light Dragoon Dress; everyone agreed it was quite shocking.' (Library and Archives Canada, C-128839)

British flank prevented them from intervening in the main fight. Both lines stood and fired; reloaded and fired; reloaded and fired, but the British received the worst of the exchange and could not close to use the bayonet, yet they refused to retire and continued firing. Private Ferguson was hit in the arm although he 'knew nothing of it until my piece fell out of my hand, and I saw the blood running down in a stream'. Reluctantly he went to the rear where wagons waited to evacuate the wounded and had his arm bandaged with his own handkerchief. Desperate for water, the officer tending him could only offer rum, and decent teetotaller that he was he accepted without enthusiasm, 'to find partial relief – the only time I ever experienced any benefit from spiritous liquors'.

After 25 minutes of this pounding Riall, his own coat pierced by a bullet as the flanks 'mouldered away like a rope of sand', was forced to order a withdrawal which was completed in good order without American pursuit, covered by the guns firing from the north bank of the Chippawa River. The battle cost 95 British and 16 Indians killed, with 321 reported wounded and 46 missing; American casualties totalled around 300 including 53 dead, in what was the most sanguinary encounter of the war so far. But most significantly, British regulars had for the first time been clearly beaten in a stand-up fight of roughly matching strength, and the Americans exalted.

'No battle could have been better arranged to test the superiority' of the two armies, thought Captain Joseph Henderson of the 22nd US Infantry, for there 'was no advantage on either side from numbers or position'; the stain of Crysler's Farm and so many previous defeats had been erased. Captain William H. Merritt, a Canadian militia officer commanding the Niagara Light

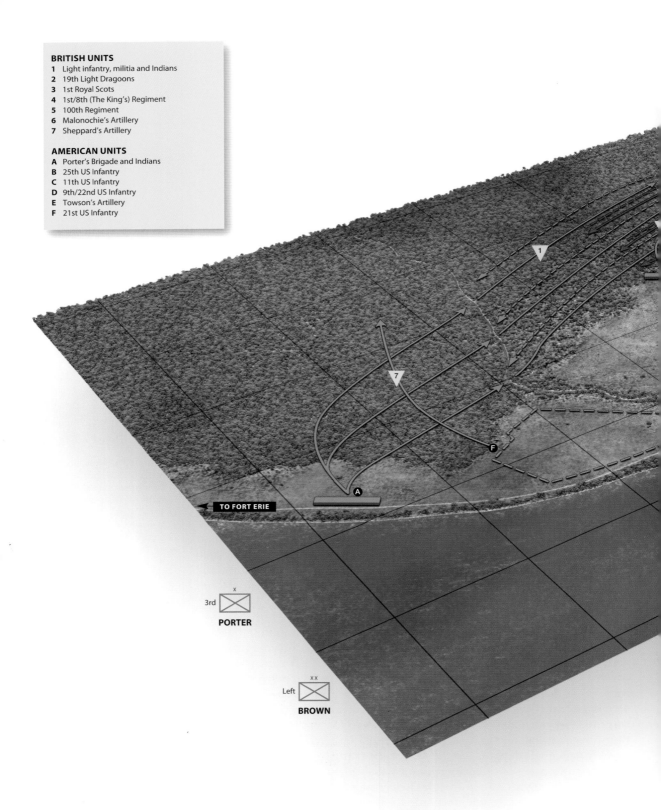

BRITISH UNITS
1 Light infantry, militia and Indians
2 19th Light Dragoons
3 1st Royal Scots
4 1st/8th (The King's) Regiment
5 100th Regiment
6 Malonochie's Artillery
7 Sheppard's Artillery

AMERICAN UNITS
A Porter's Brigade and Indians
B 25th US Infantry
C 11th US Infantry
D 9th/22nd US Infantry
E Towson's Artillery
F 21st US Infantry

← **TO FORT ERIE**

3rd ⊠ x
PORTER

Left ⊠ x x
BROWN

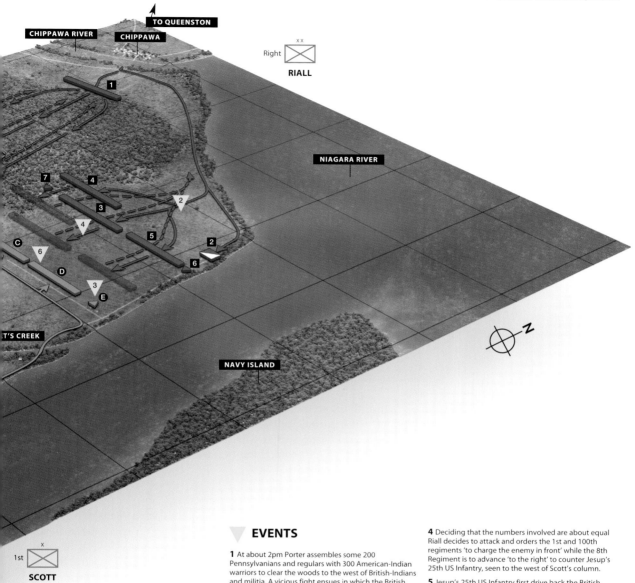

Note: Gridlines are shown at intervals of 500yds/457m

CHIPPAWA RIVER **CHIPPAWA** **TO QUEENSTON**

Right [X X] **RIALL**

NIAGARA RIVER

NAVY ISLAND

T'S CREEK

1st [X] **SCOTT**

◀ **EVENTS**

1 At about 2pm Porter assembles some 200 Pennsylvanians and regulars with 300 American-Indian warriors to clear the woods to the west of British-Indians and militia. A vicious fight ensues in which the British are driven to the north edge of the wood, where the Americans are in turn put to flight by three British light companies.

2 Some time after 3pm Riall orders the British main force across the Chippawa River, and they advance along the road in column of march as the fight rages in the woods. When they reach the northern edge of 'the Plain' they deploy, and the artillery opens fire on the America picket of Captain Benjamin Ropes at Ussher's House and barn.

3 As Scott's column emerged from cover on the south side of Street's Creek, sometime after 4pm, the British artillery switches target to engage them. They deploy quickly and efficiently while Captain Nathan Towson's guns return the British fire.

4 Deciding that the numbers involved are about equal Riall decides to attack and orders the 1st and 100th regiments 'to charge the enemy in front' while the 8th Regiment is to advance 'to the right' to counter Jesup's 25th US Infantry, seen to the west of Scott's column.

5 Jesup's 25th US Infantry first drive back the British light companies in the woods, then engage the 1st/8th Regiment in the flank, forcing it to withdraw and preventing it from joining the main fight on the Plain.

6 For almost half an hour the two lines exchange fire with the British getting the worst of it from Towson's guns and the 11th US Infantry enfilading their right flank. With Brown's permission, the American artillery commander, Major Jacob Hindman, also deploys two guns in the centre of the American line.

7 At the same time Brown orders Ripley to take the 21st US Infantry in a wide outflanking movement, but the dense undergrowth slows them. Before they can intervene, Riall orders a retreat and the British are able to retire north of the Chippawa River in good order.

CHIPPAWA, 5 JULY 1814
The British Right Division under Riall advance to confront the American Left Division under Brown south of the Chippawa River.

Battle of Chippawa. This picture by Alonzo Chappel depicts Scott ordering McNeil's 11th US Infantry to attack the British right flank. As with so many mid-century portrayals the uniforms are hopelessly inaccurate, while a dead highlander and French cuirassier have arrived miraculously from somewhere, possibly Waterloo. (Anne S. K. Brown Collection, Brown University)

Dragoons, 'candidly confessed we were beaten', and even captured British officers were effusive in their praise. 'We had never seen those grey-jackets before', said one, and 'supposed it was only a line of Militia-men, [but] it became clear enough we had something besides Militia-men to deal with.'

AN UNEASY CALM

Little happened for two days as the surgeons dealt with the aftermath of battle, until the Americans learned of a disused logging road that offered the chance to outflank Riall on the Chippawa River, and Ripley's Brigade advanced early on 8 July levering Riall out of his position and forcing him to retire on Fort George, followed by a trail of civilian refugees. The Americans occupied Queenston on 10 July where they began to receive reinforcements.

As the two armies faced each other near Fort George, Drummer Jarvis Hanks recalled the British fired a few artillery rounds at the Americans:

[Scott] was sitting on his horse, a few rods in front of the line, about noon, the soldiers lazily reclining upon their arms, some preparing and eating their dinner, when a shell was fired from the fort. In a moment we all saw it, and heard it buzzing through the air, and were all upon the lookout to ascertain where it was going to fall. Gen[era]l Scott threw up his sword in such a manner as to take sight across it, at the bomb, and found that it would fall upon him and his charger, unless he made his escape instanter. He wheeled his spirited animal to the left, and buried his spurs in his sides. The whole army was gazing upon the scene with intense anxiety for the safety of their beloved commander,

and with the highest admiration of his decision of Character in such an emergency, when the shell *actually dropped upon the very spot* he had a moment before occupied, and exploded without damage!

John Norton. The war chief of the Grand River warriors served the British extremely well to the end of the war. Afterwards he took his wife and son to Scotland where he had been educated, and though they returned to Grand River it appears that some years later Norton became estranged from his family. (LAC C-123841)

At Montreal Prevost reacted with dismay to the news of Chippawa, writing to London on 12 July that he would have to act defensively until the British could attain naval supremacy on lakes Ontario and Champlain, which he still did not anticipate before September. However, the American high command was also under strain; Brown was dissatisfied with Ripley's lack of enthusiasm and general tardiness, while Scott and his officers felt they were not receiving due recognition for their success at Chippawa. Brown had to smooth ruffled feathers, and ordered an aggressive patrols programme. Brown also hoped that Chauncey would now sail from Sackets Harbor to support him, and bring heavy guns with which to assail forts George and Niagara; but Chauncey was laid up in bed with a fever, his new ship was still not ready and the American squadron dared not leave port, prompting Brown to write in frustration on 13 July: 'For God's sake let me see you.' Navy Secretary William Jones thought the lake service had been struck by paralysis, and instructed Commodore Stephen Decatur to take over before suspending the order when he learned of Chauncey's illness. Chauncey for his part took offence at Brown's tone, and as the chances of effective inter-service cooperation receded, so did any realistic chance of significant American success in the region.

On 13 July Drummond ordered reinforcements forwards and requested further support: the 2nd/89th and flank companies of the 104th Regiment moved to York, while the Incorporated Militia Battalion of Upper Canada was sent to Fort George, then on to join Riall who, having left a strong garrison of the 41st and 100th regiments in Fort George, withdrew the remainder of his force to Twenty Mile Creek to avoid being trapped between Brown and Chauncey; there he was joined by Lieutenant-Colonel Hercules Scott and the 103rd Regiment. Meanwhile Brown drilled his men and his patrols clashed frequently with Riall's screen of Canadian militia, deployed to cover his position at Twenty Mile Creek. Soon they were 'daily skirmishing and driving in States' parties, who were plundering every house they could get at'. 'The

'Why, these are regulars by God!' The grey uniform of West Point cadets was adopted in 1816 because it wore well and was considerably cheaper than the blue one. However, its real origin is not important, as it perpetuates the memory of the Left Division. (Painting by H. C. McBarron, US Army Center of Military History)

whole population is against us', complained McFarland of the 23rd US Infantry. 'Not a foraging party but is fired on, and not infrequently returns with missing numbers.' The hostile reaction of the local population and the steady drain of casualties this caused led the American to seek reprisals with the burning of property, and the whole campaign began to take a distinctly bitter tone. On 18 July the village of St David's was put to the torch, completely destroying the 40 or so houses and much to Brown's disgust; he dismissed the officer responsible, Lieutenant-Colonel Isaac W. Stone of the New York volunteer battalion, despite the latter's denial of responsibility.

A failed reconnaissance three days earlier towards Fort George, and Riall's refusal to be drawn forwards into contact led Brown to decide that without heavy guns forts George and Mississauga could not be taken. On 22 July Brown pulled back to Queenston only to find it occupied by some Canadian militia, who were roundly abused by 'King Joe' Willcocks and his men. That day Drummond arrived at York with the 2nd/89th Regiment where he received Riall's dispatch, and was alarmed by the desperate supply situation that necessitated the evacuation of civilians and putting Indian families on half rations. Riall was uncertain what to do and was anxious for Drummond's arrival; instead Drummond sent Riall detailed instructions to make a demonstration against Queenston, but not to engage the Americans until he arrived himself.

With the forts well defended Brown summoned a council of war where it was agreed to bypass them and make a risky move towards Burlington Heights at the far end of the peninsula. Brown was confident he could win the battle that he knew must follow such a move, and regarded the risks it entailed to be entirely logistical. On 24 July he suddenly retired to Chippawa, to divest himself of excess baggage, his numbers now reduced to 2,644 effectives. His plan was to bring supplies across the Niagara River from Fort Schlosser, then make an advance across country towards

Burlington. But he had not counted on British reaction to his moves, and when Riall heard of Brown's withdrawal he immediately sent Pearson south to shadow him.

Pearson's 2nd, or Light Brigade, comprised the Glengarry Light Infantry and Incorporated Militia of Upper Canada, and he also had under command a detachment of 19th Light Dragoons and the 1st Militia Brigade under Lieutenant-Colonel Love Parry, supported by two 6-pdrs and a 5½in. howitzer – a total of around 1,100 men. At dawn on 25 July they marched through the ruins of St David's and halted at Lundy's Lane, a road about one-and-a-half kilometres north of Niagara Falls which ran east–west from the Portage Road at the village of the same name – after a Pennsylvania Loyalist who had settled there in 1786 – where he was joined by John Norton and his warriors. At this point the British were outnumbered by the Americans to their south, but Riall arrived that afternoon, while the 1st Brigade under Hercules Scott, with five companies of the 1st/8th and seven of the 103rd Regiment, the 2nd Militia Brigade, and the reserve comprising seven companies of 1st Royal Scots under Lieutenant-Colonel John Gordon, approached from Twelve Mile Creek via Beaver Dams.

LUNDY'S LANE

In the morning Drummond reached Fort George from York on the schooner *Netley*, accompanied by the 2nd/89th Regiment under Lieutenant-Colonel Joseph Morrison in the *Star* and *Charwell*; he sent them to join Riall. He then organized a force of 500 men under Colonel John Tucker of the 41st Regiment, supported by a party of Indians, to sortie from Fort Niagara, while armed seamen in boats under Captain Alexander Dobbs RN also gave support from the river. When Tucker scattered the New York militia and found Lewiston abandoned, Drummond ordered him to return to Fort Niagara with part of his force while the rest, including the Indians, crossed over to the Canadian shore at about 3pm. This force might have accomplished more had Tucker remained on the American bank to threaten Black Rock and Buffalo, but

Major Thomas Sidney Jesup, US Army (1788–1860). Thomas Jesup, commanding the 25th US Infantry, was appointed Quartermaster General after the war and held the post for no less than 42 years, becoming the 'father' of the modern Quartermaster Corps. (Portrait by Charles Bird King, Washington National Cathedral, Bequest of Mary Jesup Sitgreaves)

LEFT
Captain Wilson saved by a squaw. This fanciful depiction by George Jones RA, shows Captain John Wilson of the Royal Scots wounded on the Chippawa battlefield, supposedly having been attacked by an Indian whom he killed, then saved by an Indian woman from the nearby village. (Royal Scots Museum, Edinburgh)

although he knew it meant his supply base at Fort Schlosser was threatened, when Brown gained news of this movement he was unperturbed, and boldly decided that the best way to turn round the British advance was to advance himself towards Queenston: he sent for Winfield Scott.

At about the same time Drummond sent Morrison on to Lundy's Lane with some 800 men comprising his own 2nd/89th Regiment and the light companies of the 1st Royal Scots, 1st/8th and 41st regiments, Maclachlan's 24-pdr detachment and a Royal Marine Artillery rocket section, plus a large body of Indians. Late in the afternoon Winfield Scott arrived at Lundy's Lane. Having deciding that the British on the hill opposite were of similar numbers he deployed his men into line and prepared to attack. As the Americans approached, but before they debouched from the woods to his front, a now-nervous Riall thought the entire of Brown's force – reputedly 5,000 men – was bearing down on him, and he decided to retire on Queenston. Riall ordered a retreat, only for Drummond to arrive shortly afterwards and countermand this order, and although there is no record of their conversation, towards 7pm they rode back onto the position.

Drummond put some 1,600 men into line along the hill that dominated the junction between Lundy's Lane and the Portage Road with the 24-pdrs, 6-pdrs and Congreve rocket detachment deployed forward of the crest of the rise. When Scott's men emerged from the wood at about 7pm he was shocked to find the British in strength and ready to stand, and at first considered retiring. Instead he gamely chose to deploy his brigade and stand fast, but in doing so they came under heavy fire from the British guns which hit the 22nd US Infantry particularly hard. Nonetheless they formed line and opened fire on the British to their front, despite the extreme range of some 450m. As at Chippawa, Scott was supported by Towson's guns although this time they were far less effective, for the British guns were in contrast, ideally situated to wreak fearful damage, and Americans fell steadily to round shot and shell – there being little of the very effective shrapnel available in the Niagara Peninsula.

Scott's Brigade stoically endured this punishment and stood its ground for some 45 minutes, until Scott decided he had to advance. But the order was then cancelled after about 100m leaving the American line still some 400m distant of the British. Meanwhile, accompanied by the unmistakable sounds of battle that carried to Buffalo 32km away, word reached Brown's camp near Chippawa that Scott was engaged with some 1,100 British. Ever bold, Brown immediately set his men marching towards the gunfire.

A few kilometres to the north the British column under Hercules Scott, marching from Twelve Mile Creek via Beaver Dams towards the battle, could also hear 'the roar of Artillery and of Musketry pealing in Our front, sometimes rattling in heavy surges – sometimes scant, as if the troops pressed were retiring'. The noise was phenomenal noted Elihu H. Shepard, recalling how it 'is difficult to bring the imagination to realize the tremendous roar of the Falls of Niagara, the thunder of the artillery, the crash of musketry, and the shouts of battle …'

On Drummond's right the Canadian 1st Militia Brigade and the Glengarry Light Infantry noted the American advance exposed their left flank, and when, together with some of Norton's Indians, they moved forwards to engage it, Drummond ordered three companies of 1st Royal Scots forwards in support. Seeing the danger Scott in turn ordered the 11th US Infantry on his left to wheel and face the threat, but the volleys with which they returned the skirmishers' fire had little effect on the scattered Canadians and Indians; and far worse, as well as having suffered severe casualties from the British guns. Scott's ineffective firing for so long from extreme range had the inevitable effect that his men were now running short of ammunition.

However, with twilight descending the 25th US Infantry under Jesup on Scott's right found a track that enabled him to advance his regiment under cover to attack the British left flank. Jesup was born in West Virginia and raised in Kentucky, and after being commissioned in 1808 had served as adjutant general to Major-General William Hull being taken prisoner at the surrender of Detroit, but later exchanged. Led by Captain Daniel Ketchum's company, who were equipped and drilled to act as skirmishers, the Americans fired a volley that took the Incorporated Militia and the Light Company of the 1st/8th Regiment stationed there by surprise and then advanced, overrunning the two easternmost companies of Incorporated Militia and seriously wounding their commanding officer, Lieutenant-Colonel William Robinson.

LEFT
Marching towards Lundy's Lane. Among the units that reinforced Drummond was the 103rd Regiment, largely composed of very young men and boys and suffering from disciplinary problems. Fortunately their commanding officer, 39-year-old Hercules Scott, was an experienced and effective officer. (Drawing by George Balbar, courtesy of Haunted Press)

RIGHT
Drummond turns the troops back to Lundy's Lane. When Drummond learned of Riall's withdrawal he spurred his horse and galloped past two retreating columns, turning them south before meeting the Incorporated Militia Battalion at Muddy Run Creek, some three kilometres north of Lundy's Lane, and halting it. (Drawing by George Balbar, courtesy of Haunted Press)

Brown's advance to Lundy's Lane

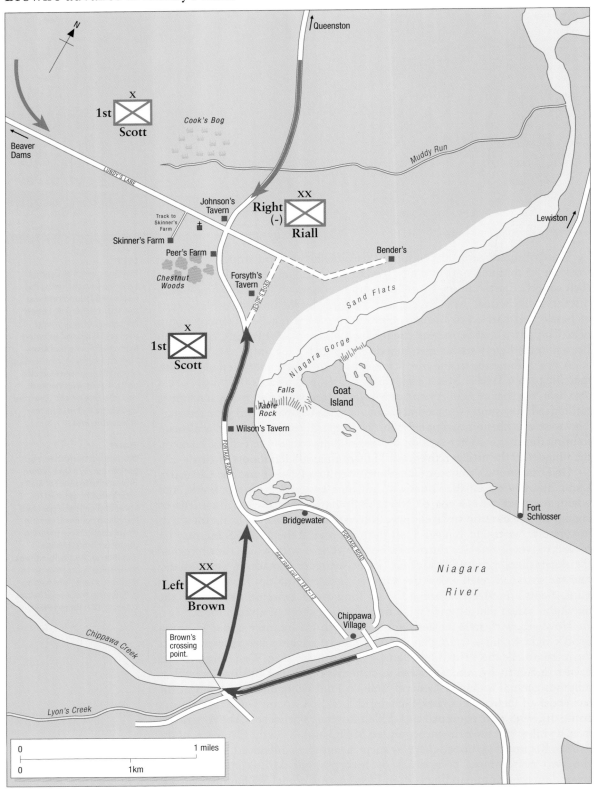

N

Queenston

Cook's Bog

Muddy Run

1st
Scott

Beaver
Dams

LUNDY'S LANE

Johnson's
Tavern

Right
(-)
Riall

Track to
Skinner's
Farm

Skinner's Farm

Peer's Farm

Bender's

Lewiston

Chestnut
Woods

Forsyth's
Tavern

Sand Flats

1st
Scott

Niagara Gorge

Falls

Goat
Island

Table
Rock

Wilson's Tavern

Portage Road

Bridgewater

Fort
Schlosser

Left
Brown

Niagara
River

Chippawa
Village

Chippawa Creek

Brown's
crossing
point.

Lyon's Creek

0		1 miles
0	1km	

46

MANDERS

As the remaining militia fired and retreated to form a new line almost at a right angle to the main British position, Major Robert Lisle's squadron of 19th Light Dragoons also retired, leaving Drummond's left flank hanging in the air. Jesup pressed on towards the Portage Road and his regiment also formed up almost at a right angle to Lundy's Lane itself. Jesup again selected Ketchum's Company to secure the road junction and reconnoitre, and Ketchum's men soon began to capture small groups of British and Canadians using the road. Riall had been wounded in the right arm and was riding slowly back with his orderly when he too was taken, followed shortly afterwards by an aide of Drummond's sent to fetch back Lisle's dragoons; then Captain William H. Merritt was captured on his way to report the situation to Drummond.

Jesup could see the muzzle flashes of the British guns in the descending darkness, but with a dozen officers and over 100 soldier prisoners to contend with he could not attack them. He therefore chose to send Ketchum to the rear with the prisoners and, shortly afterwards, received word that the rest of the brigade had been cut to pieces. By 8.30pm Scott's Brigade had indeed been reduced to around 600 men, and the fight subsided in the gloom with only Maclachlan's gunners remaining in action. Drummond had reason to feel satisfied, believing that he had maintained his position against Brown's entire force despite Hercules Scott having not yet arrived, as he quickly marched the 19km that separated them.

Drummond was, however, taking no chances; he retired and realigned his line slightly, but despite the failing light he left the guns forwards of the infantry line. And as the 25th US Infantry groped towards the rear Brown

LEFT
Rocket section, Royal Marine Artillery. The Royal Marine Artillery detachment serving with Drummond's force was equipped with two notoriously inaccurate 12-pdr Congreve rockets. But they had already demonstrated their value in the defence of La Colle Mills. (From *Military Uniforms in America. Years of Growth, 1796–1851* © The Company of Military Historians, 1977)

RIGHT
Private, 104th (New Brunswick) Regiment of Foot. Besides Canadians, Britons and 200 Acadians from New Brunswick, Nova Scotia and Prince Edward Island, by 1812 the 104th (New Brunswick) Regiment included Americans from New York, New Jersey and Pennsylvania, Germans, Italians, Poles and Swedes, and some Indians and Africans. (Painting by Don Troiani, www.historicalimagebank.com)

arrived with the rest of the American force while Hercules Scott's men arrived at about the same time – to be greeted by a cheer from the British line – and the three 6-pdrs under Captain James Mackonochie RA were sent forwards to join Maclachlan, just as the British guns finally ceased firing.

Immediately Brown prepared to renew the battle; he ordered Ripley's 2nd Brigade to deploy forwards of Scott's 1st, and both Brown and Ripley decided the hill where the British guns were stationed was the key to the British position. Ripley deployed the 1st US Infantry to form a line facing the British infantry and draw their attention and Brown ordered the 21st US Infantry, commanded by Colonel James Miller, to attack the hill. Miller, tall and physically imposing, 'raised his herculean form and fixed his eye, for an instant, intently upon the battery; then turning his bit of tobacco', gave a reply that would become a stock of American schoolboy legend: 'I'll try, Sir!' But before he could do so 1st US Infantry, although amounting to just three companies of 150 men in total, advanced towards it.

As the smoke was now clearing and the moon rising, the British guns opened fire, and, soon realizing that there 'was no possibility of my annoying the enemy and a certainty of destroying my men', the commanding officer, Lieutenant-Colonel Robert C. Nicholas, wisely ordered them to 'right about face' and retire to the base of the hill. Suddenly at about 9.15pm, having moved silently in dead ground up the hill in a two-rank line with their bayonets at the 'charge', the 21st US Infantry appeared, unimpeded – indeed undetected – by British skirmishers, and halted at an old rail fence barely 30m from the guns. Throwing down the fence they fired a volley and charged, catching the British completely by surprise. Maclachlan was among the 20 or so casualties as the Americans set about the startled British gunners with the bayonet and the survivors either fled or surrendered. Morrison's 2nd/89th Regiment formed just north of the lane behind the guns was thrown into confusion as some of the artillery horses stampeded in panic through his line.

ATTACK OF MILLER'S 21ST US INFANTRY AT LUNDY'S LANE

John Norton was conversing with two officers when they noticed the Americans, and as he approached them he 'observed the Moon glimmer faintly on the plates of their Caps, the form of which denounced them to be our Enemies [American shako plates were rectangular while British shako plates were slightly curved with scalloped corners] – before I could speak, they fired'. Miller's stunning coup seized the initiative for the Americans which they never lost during the battle, and earned him the epithet 'Hero of Lundy's Lane'. Following the war the 21st US Infantry was consolidated with five others (the 4th, 9th, 13th, 40th and 46th) to form the new 5th US Infantry on 15 May 1815 under Miller's command and he was made a brigadier-general, but left the army in 1819 to serve as territorial Governor of Arkansas until 1825, where Miller County is named after him. He was elected to the United States House of Representatives in 1824 but refused the seat and became Customs Collector for Salem and Beverly (MA).

He died of a stroke in 1850 at Temple, New Hampshire. His regiment operated along the vast new frontier until the Mexican War erupted in 1846 and served under General Zachary Taylor driving the Mexicans out of Texas. It then joined General Winfield Scott in his offensive into Mexico and stormed the fortress walls of Chapultepec with lieutenants James Longstreet and George Pickett carrying the regimental colours, while Lieutenant Thomas 'Stonewall' Jackson's battery provided artillery support, all of whom would subsequently gain fame during the Civil War.

The 21st US infantry **(1)** are advancing in a line two deep, bayonets fixed 'at the charge' and led by an officer **(2)**, towards the British gunline, which they have caught by surprise having made a covered approach in the gathering darkness. A British 6-pdr **(3)** stands in the foreground while a gunner **(4)** raises the alarm.

Battle of Lundy's Lane: view from the British lines. Having been driven down from the high ground the British had to reorganize themselves before they could assault the heights. This view depicts them advancing during one of several attempts made during the night to regain the position. (From an engraving in *Harper's Magazine*, 1866, Lundy's Lane Museum)

Drummond, who was close by, ordered Morrison to counterattack and he quickly complied, opening a sharp fire at the 21st US Infantry. But the 2nd/89th's advance was hindered by guns, trees, wagons and gravestones as they crossed the cemetery to their front, and the Americans returned their fire. The two regiments had faced each other at Crysler's Farm, but this time it was the British who withdrew first, although in good order, before returning to the attack supported by three companies of 1st Royal Scots and the Light Company of the 41st Regiment. A second firefight ensued in which Morrison was among the wounded.

Once again the British retired as the 21st held their ground; once more they returned to renew the fight, and this time Drummond, whose horse had already been shot from under him, was among the wounded as a ball entered under the right ear and lodged in the back of his neck. Despite losing a great deal of blood he remained in action as the 41st's Light Company under Captain Joseph Glew briefly regained the guns. But he could not bring them away to safety for lack of horses. Once more the British withdrew, this time not to return, and with contact between the two armies now broken, Miller and his men awaited support from the main American line.

The first unit to arrive was 1st US Infantry. However, while the 21st had been performing its sterling service in securing the British gun line, the other regiment of Ripley's Brigade, the 23rd US Infantry, was advancing in column on the left and was just about to deploy into line when it was ambushed. Private Amasiah Ford recalled that 'out of 32 in the first platoon, only eight of us escaped the desperate slaughter'. Among the dead was Major Daniel McFarland, the commanding officer, throwing the regiment into confusion. Only Ripley's presence enabled the remaining officers to regain control, and they now climbed the hill to join their sister unit, shortly joined by four 6-pdrs and two 5½in howitzers. Jesup and the 25th US Infantry had also returned to the fray, and Porter's militia brigade began to arrive as Brown also appeared.

Unsure what the British intended he appears to have prevented the removal of the British guns, and was very nearly captured himself going

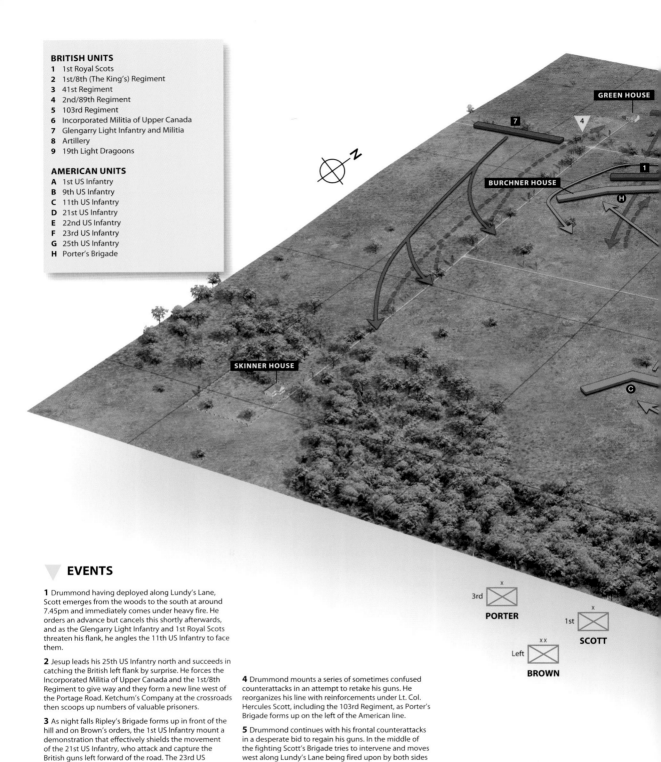

BRITISH UNITS
1   1st Royal Scots
2   1st/8th (The King's) Regiment
3   41st Regiment
4   2nd/89th Regiment
5   103rd Regiment
6   Incorporated Militia of Upper Canada
7   Glengarry Light Infantry and Militia
8   Artillery
9   19th Light Dragoons

AMERICAN UNITS
A   1st US Infantry
B   9th US Infantry
C   11th US Infantry
D   21st US Infantry
E   22nd US Infantry
F   23rd US Infantry
G   25th US Infantry
H   Porter's Brigade

GREEN HOUSE

BURCHNER HOUSE

SKINNER HOUSE

3rd
PORTER

1st
SCOTT

Left
BROWN

▼ EVENTS

1 Drummond having deployed along Lundy's Lane, Scott emerges from the woods to the south at around 7.45pm and immediately comes under heavy fire. He orders an advance but cancels this shortly afterwards, and as the Glengarry Light Infantry and 1st Royal Scots threaten his flank, he angles the 11th US Infantry to face them.

2 Jesup leads his 25th US Infantry north and succeeds in catching the British left flank by surprise. He forces the Incorporated Militia of Upper Canada and the 1st/8th Regiment to give way and they form a new line west of the Portage Road. Ketchum's Company at the crossroads then scoops up numbers of valuable prisoners.

3 As night falls Ripley's Brigade forms up in front of the hill and on Brown's orders, the 1st US Infantry mount a demonstration that effectively shields the movement of the 21st US Infantry, who attack and capture the British guns left forward of the road. The 23rd US Infantry support them on their right, and in due course the 1st US Infantry on their left.

4 Drummond mounts a series of sometimes confused counterattacks in an attempt to retake his guns. He reorganizes his line with reinforcements under Lt. Col. Hercules Scott, including the 103rd Regiment, as Porter's Brigade forms up on the left of the American line.

5 Drummond continues with his frontal counterattacks in a desperate bid to regain his guns. In the middle of the fighting Scott's Brigade tries to intervene and moves west along Lundy's Lane being fired upon by both sides until it breaks in confusion and re-forms west of Porter's position.

LUNDY'S LANE, 25 JULY 1814

The American invasion force attempts to storm the British position along Lundy's Lane in a night action, with Scott's 1st Brigade suffering heavy casualties.

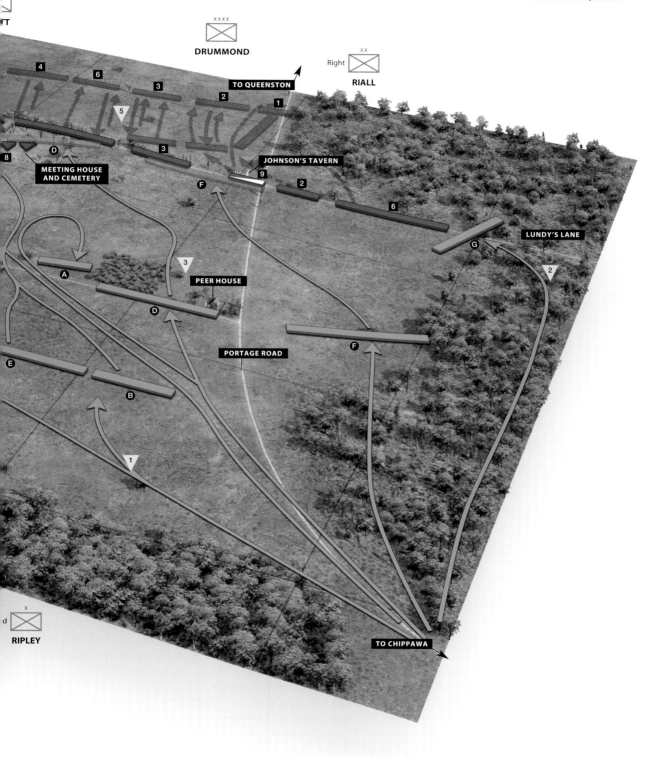

Note: Gridlines are shown at intervals of 250yds/228m

DRUMMOND

Right RIALL

TO QUEENSTON

4

6

3

2

1

5

D

3

3

8

MEETING HOUSE
AND CEMETERY

JOHNSON'S TAVERN

F

9

2

6

LUNDY'S LANE

3

G

2

A

PEER HOUSE

D

F

E

PORTAGE ROAD

B

1

TO CHIPPAWA

RIPLEY

Scott wounded. In intensity if not in scale the close-quarter fighting matched anything the British had faced in the Peninsula. It led to a particularly high casualty rate among senior officers of both sides, including Winfield Scott. (D. H. Strother, *Illustrated Life of General Winfield Scott*, 1847)

forwards to look. Realizing that the British were about to renew the attack, he quickly ordered Porter to deploy to Ripley's left; Porter was only just in time. Drummond knew that he must recapture his guns or be left unable to face the Americans on the open field; it was imperative that the British counterattack at the earliest opportunity, but with many disordered units his army was in a jumbled confusion and he would have to re-form it first – a difficult task in the darkness.

He decided to arrange them into a single line divided into two wings – as all the while 'the ridiculous mistakes which could only occur fighting an army speaking the same language were laughable though serious – Who goes there? – A friend – To whom? – To King George. If the appellants, as you would call them, were of that persuasion [sic], all was well, but when a friend to Madison, then there was a difference of opinion.' Consequently both sides benefited from windfalls as messages and prisoners fell into their hands, but there were also frequent 'friendly fire' incidents on both sides. It took Drummond some 30 minutes before he was ready to launch the counterattack, yet now he compounded his failure to protect the guns with light infantry by failing to use them ahead of the assault.

The British and Canadian line moved forwards at about 10pm with two companies of Incorporated Militia and the Light Company of the 41st Regiment on the right, 1st Royal Scots and the 2nd/89th Regiment in the centre, while the right flank comprised two more companies of Incorporated Militia and the Light Company of the 1st/8th Regiment. The lull had enabled the Americans to reorganize as well, and they were ready, but they had also neglected to post skirmishers to their front. As the British approached, both sides were in perfect silence. The Americans had orders to fire second so the British would be illuminated by their muzzle flashes, but as the first volley crashed along the line, fired from within 30m or even as close as ten, it caused horrific casualties and greatly reduced the effectiveness of the American reply; it also knocked down so many gunners that it effectively neutralized the American artillery. But it did not break their line, and another fierce firefight started with both sides loading and firing as rapidly as possible.

Drummond and Ripley rode up and down behind their respective lines, exhorting and encouraging their men; Drummond shouting 'Stick to them, my fine fellows', matched by the more practical American cry of 'Level low

Aftermath of the battle of Lundy's Lane. William Dunlop noted the unenviable situation of an army surgeon after a battle 'surrounded by suffering, pain and misery, much of which he knows it is not in his power to heal or even to assuage'. (Drawing by George Balbar, courtesy of Haunted Press).

and fire at their flashes.' After another 25 minutes of pounding and seeing that the Americans remained unshaken, Drummond gave the command for the British line to withdraw which they did maintaining good order. Ripley knew they would be back and as his men closed their gaps he ordered Porter's men up to extend his line to the left.

At about 10.45pm the British renewed the attack, once more closing to a range of some 30m in the darkness as a 'sheet of fire' saw the fight begin once more, this time 'more severe, and … longer continued than the last'. And this time the Americans began to waver; Porter's Brigade was disordered and fired only irregularly before starting to withdraw, and the 23rd US Infantry in the centre also began to give way. Winfield Scott now tried to intervene with his brigade by an assault on the British line in column, but in the dark it immediately came under fire from both lines suffering heavy casualties and withdrew westwards in some disorder. The firefight continued and then gradually died down, the British being too exhausted to press the attack with the bayonet. Significantly, Lieutenant John Le Couteur would never forget that Drummond 'rode up to the 103rd [Regiment]. "My lads *will you* charge the Americans?" He *put a question* instead of *giving the order* – they fired instead of charging.' Instead, the British again retired down the bloody slope.

Despite Drummond having inflicted heavy casualties on the Americans, he was still no nearer to reclaiming his guns, and he ordered a third attack. Shortly before 11.30pm the British and Canadians advanced once more in a repetition of the same blunt frontal assault that had proved unsuccessful thus far. But having now re-formed his brigade, Winfield Scott also chose to attack once more, and this time the result was even worse for the battered remnants of his command. As it crossed the front of Lieutenant-Colonel William

Drummond's 104th Regiment they poured volleys into the Americans until they retreated. Out of some 900 men that Scott brought to the field, barely 100 were still in formation.

Soon afterwards Brown was wounded by a musket ball in the thigh and his aide was killed. Brown was then wounded again, but refused to depart the field as he watched the third British attack come in. Once more heavy firing commenced but in the dark the British did not close, and Porter decided to attack; he forced them to give way and took a number of prisoners, while on the right the 25th US Infantry also went well. Winfield Scott appeared beside Jesup and was knocked unconscious and Jesup received his fourth wound of the action but, seemingly indestructible, he stayed on the field.

However, it was in the centre that the fight would be decided, and here the British appeared to have finally broken through as the 2nd/89th Regiment got amongst the guns and a vicious hand-to-hand fight developed. But as the troops on their flanks pulled back so those in the centre were also forced to give way, and sometime after midnight the Americans were left once more in possession of the heights. Drummond's third attack had failed, although his report written three days later tried to obfuscate this by claiming the guns were recaptured, along with an American 5½in. howitzer and a 6-pdr, and 'in limbering up our Guns at one period, one of the Enemy's Six pounders was put, by mistake, upon a limber of ours, and one of our six limbered on one of his, by which means the pieces were exchanged, and thus, we have gained only one Gun'.

This was a serious case of gilding the lily after the event, because the stark truth was that at this stage the Americans retained control of all the ordnance on the hill. Brown had been forced to leave the field and ordered Ripley to gather the wounded and retire. Ripley waited for around 30 minutes until he was sure the British would not return, then ordered Porter's Brigade to take off the guns. But exhaustion coupled with the absence of horses or harness meant the Americans only succeeded in taking away one. Otherwise the exhausted and battered American force was able to withdraw to their camp unmolested by the equally shattered British and Canadians, who withdrew down the hill and slept on their arms amid rumours that the Americans would be back. Only when it was known for certain that the Americans had gone did they relax, until it began to grow light towards 5am and the full horror of the night's work was revealed.

Hundreds of men lay sprawled dead, dying or horribly wounded and groaning for water. The Americans lost 173 killed, 571 wounded and 117 missing, some 45 per cent of those engaged; only two officers and 30 men of 22nd US Infantry marched into camp that night. American Surgeon William E. Horner 'had sole attendance and dressing of one hundred and seventy-three sick and wounded. Fingers became so sore from incessant dabbing in water and pus that I could seize nothing without pain.' British losses were officially stated as 84 killed – Lieutenant H. N. Moorsom of the 104th, 'a very intelligent and promising young officer', according to Drummond, was killed by one of the last shots fired – 559 men were wounded including Drummond, and 193 were missing including Riall, although it seems likely this last figure was overstated, and represents total losses of about 30 per cent of those engaged.

On the British side Surgeon William Dunlop of the 2nd/89th Regiment was among those left to pick up the pieces as the miserable British wounded were brought into Fort George, where he had the assistance of only a sergeant, in charge of a hospital with 320 patients, noting 'There is hardly on the face of the earth a less enviable situation than that of an Army Surgeon after a battle – worn out and fatigued in body and mind, surrounded by suffering, pain and misery, much of which he knows it is not in his power to heal or even to assuage.' Among the melancholy scenes he witnessed was the wife of an American prisoner who came to nurse her husband, 'lying on a truss of straw, writhing in agony, for his sufferings were most dreadful'. Dunlop watched as the poor woman took her man's head in her lap and wept, until awakened by a groan from her unfortunate husband, she clasped her hands, and looking wildly around, exclaimed, 'O that the King and President were both here this moment to see the misery their quarrels lead to – they surely would not go to war without cause that they could give as a reason to God at the last day, for thus destroying the creatures that He hath made in his own image.'

As with other branches of medical science the art of surgery was crude indeed, amounting to little more than an attempt, if possible, to extract the bullet or shell fragment followed by cleaning and dressing of wounds; internal surgery was practically impossible. Wounds in the arm or leg would receive similar treatment with splinting of broken bones if not complicated, but amputation was usually necessary, with precious little anaesthetic. Amputation was also likely for the reason that it converted a difficult wound into a relatively simple one, and made life easier for massively overworked medical staff; but antisepsis was unheard of and little attention was paid to hygiene of either persons or buildings, so it is unsurprising that expected mortality rates for simple fractures was nine per cent, of compound or open fractures 42 per cent, and from gunshot wounds up to 50 per cent.

Later the wounded were transferred to York but the general hospital was too small to accommodate them and the many sick, so other buildings including a church had to be taken over; but men evacuated to York were debilitated by the journey and less likely to recover. At least the methods of transport were marginally better than those found in Europe, where the poor wounded were frequently jolted and bounced to death in any available unsprung country wagons that could be pressed into service. In America they were more variously carried on litters made of blankets strung between poles; or by water, as well as by wagons and sleighs. As for the dead, there were so many that they had to be burned rather than buried. Private Shadrach Byfield of the 41st Regiment recalled that one Indian persisted in trying to throw a wounded American onto the fire, despite being repeatedly restrained by Byfield's mates. Eventually they lost patience with the obstinate native; they shot him, and threw him onto the fire.

Ripley realized that although the British might expect reinforcement the Americans could not, and, on the morning of 26 July, acting in direct contravention of Brown's orders, he withdrew the American force to the Black Rock Ferry site, retreating as soon as his men had thrown excess stores into the river and destroyed Street Mills and the bridge at Chippawa. In his superb account, Donald Graves concludes that while Lundy's Lane was a tactical victory for the Americans, their subsequent failure to secure the British guns they had captured and exploit their position rendered it an operational success for the British. But regardless of the final balance of victory, after performing conspicuously poorly during the first two years of war the US Army had finally shown the determination, fortitude, and discipline that had previously been lacking.

Yet despite the pride they could take in their resilient performance in the field, once again the overall American effort proved to be too little and too late: they had been unable to overwhelm the British defences in the Niagara, even though these had yet to receive the reinforcements from Europe that both sides knew were on their way. And it was not until 5 August that Chauncey appeared off Fort George ready to contest the lake, too late to affect the outcome; throughout the war had run a theme that both sides would gain control on the water at the wrong time to assist offensive operations along the lakeshore.

CONJOCTA CREEK

At the end of July Ripley was in favour of withdrawal across the river, the American force now being reduced to barely 2,100 effectives and with no prospect of significant reinforcement. But Brown insisted that Fort Erie must be held, although it was still less a fort than a fortified bridgehead, and the Americans worked feverishly to improve their toehold on Canadian territory. The unfinished earthworks were eminently vulnerable, and had Drummond followed up closely after the battle and forced the Americans to fight again, he might have been able to bounce them out of the peninsula before they had time to consolidate themselves.

Fortunately for Brown, Drummond decided not to follow up immediately, but instead withdrew the 11km to Queenston to await reinforcements; there he released his local militia to ease the logistic burden, and sent the 41st, 2nd/89th and 100th regiments to the forts to shorten his supply line. This backward step would doom the British to six weeks of intense and bloody frustration, for by the time he began his pursuit Drummond knew that with only 3,000 men he was too weak for sustained operations against prepared positions at Fort Erie. So in an attempt to draw the defenders out by cutting off their supplies, Drummond sent a force of 580 men to destroy the depots at Buffalo and Black Rock, hoping this would provoke a response.

The force comprised six companies of the 41st, the 2nd/89th Light Company and the flank companies of the 104th Regiment, under Colonel Tucker of the 41st. Tucker, whose nickname was 'Brigadier Shindy', was not well respected – 'Shindy' was slang for a dance suggesting he was flighty and unreliable. Despite crossing the river unopposed on the night of 2/3 August he did nothing for four hours, then advanced without advance or flank guards. At Conjocta (also known as Conjocheta or Scajaquada) Creek the British met a strong detachment of 1st US Rifle Regiment out from Black Rock, some 240 men supported by a few militia and volunteers, commanded by Major Ludowick Morgan, who had taken down the bridge and occupied a breastwork on the far bank.

As the British approached the bridge the Americans held their fire until it was so effective that the 41st Regiment recoiled; thereafter the remainder of Tucker's force advanced towards the riflemen who kept up such an effective fire that the attackers could find no other means to cross, despite the creek being fordable a kilometre and a half upstream. Tucker blamed the men who he claimed, 'displayed an unpardonable degree of unsteadiness', prompting him to retreat after three hours without achieving his objectives after losing 11 killed, 17 wounded and four missing, against two Americans killed and eight wounded. On the American side Lieutenant Jonathan Kearsley noted that 'the skill in planning and the firmness in the execution of the riflemen defeated the designs of the British and saved the entire American army'.

FORT ERIE

Drummond's light troops did not drive in the American pickets and draw up to Fort Erie until 3 August, five days after Brown made the decision to hold it. Finally able to examine the defences he was furious at Tucker's failure to lever the Americans out of Canada, and issued a severe censure to the troops in a general order that forbade 'crouching, ducking or laying down when advancing under fire', against riflemen or not. He then sent the 41st Regiment back to the forts to be replaced by the Régiment de Watteville. This was one of two Swiss mercenary units in British service that reached Canada in mid-1813. The uniforms were standard British pattern and the men, noted William Dunlop, consisting of all the nationalities of Europe, 'greatly excelled themselves in gastronomic lore; and thus while our fellows had no better shift than to frizzle their rations of salt provisions on the ends of their ramrods, these being practical botanists, sent out one soldier from each mess, who gathered a haversack full of pot herbs, which, with a little flour, their ration was converted into a capital kettle of soup'.

Now in front of Fort Erie, but with his supply line stretching back 64km to the mouth of the Niagara and threatened by Chauncey's American squadron on Lake Ontario, Drummond was in a difficult position. But the critical failure had been his own tardy advance; he now had no option but to attack the American position directly, and what he saw was far from reassuring. The Americans had been strengthening the fort since its capture and it now covered some 12ha with a 730m line of defensive works roughly parallel to the lake, just east of the fort, and a battery near the shore, with another battery on a sand mound called Snake Hill in the south-western corner of the position. Besides some 18 guns comprising its defences the approaches were covered by batteries at Black Rock and by three US Navy schooners on the lake under Lieutenant Augustus Conklin USN, while the garrison could be supplied and reinforced from the opposite shore, making it altogether an 'ugly customer'. To make matters worse rain began falling soon after the British invested the fort and continued almost ceaselessly for the next month.

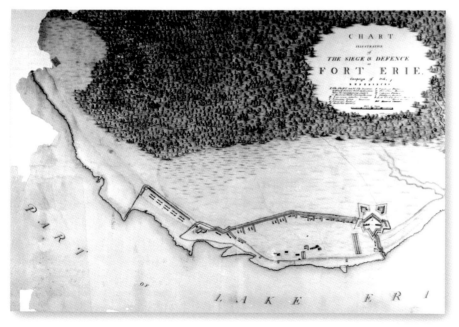

'Chart of Siege and Defense of Fort Erie, 1814'. This contemporary map shows the extent of the American defences to the south of the fort itself. Most of the perimeter was protected with a ditch and abatis and was constructed under the direction of Lt. Col. Eleazar D. Wood. (US Army Corps of Engineers)

RIGHT
The Régiment de Watteville was formed in 1801 from the remains of four Swiss regiments raised by the British for service in the Austrian Army. It served in the Mediterranean including the battle of Maida in July 1806. (From *Military Uniforms in America. Years of Growth, 1796–1851* © The Company of Military Historians, 1977)

Brigadier-General Edmund Pendleton Gaines, US Army (1777–1849). After the war when Jacob Brown, US Commanding General, died in 1828, Gaines and Winfield Scott were the two ranking generals who could have been considered to succeed him. However, they had publicly quarrelled with each other, and Alexander Macomb was promoted over them both. (Toronto Public Library, T-352)

On 5 August, Brigadier-General Edmund P. Gaines arrived to assume command from the wounded Brown while the British camped in woods about three kilometres to the north, and Ripley loyally reverted to command of his brigade in the Snake Hill area in the south. Gaines was a Virginian whose family moved to North Carolina after the Revolutionary War. He enlisted in the army in 1799 and in 1807, as commandant of Fort Stoddert, he arrested Aaron Burr and testified at his trial. Following leave of absence from the army to practise law he returned in 1812. He was with William Henry Harrison at the battle of the Thames, and commanded the 25th US Infantry at Crysler's Farm with distinction.

The now-cautious Drummond decided not to risk an assault on the fort until he had weakened it, and sent to Fort George for heavy guns. By 1814 British siege doctrine was well established, but unfortunately Drummond lacked experienced engineer officers – there were only 19 in all British North America – and there was little by way of action while his young and very inexperienced engineer, Lieutenant George Philpott RE, completed the construction of a battery armed with three 24-pdr guns, a 24-pdr carronade and an 8in. mortar.

Skirmishing around the fort continued as the Americans tried to slow down the siege process; Morgan's 1st US Rifles were augmented by Captain Benjamin Birdsall's two companies of 4th US Rifles who went into the woods on 6, 10 and 12 August, although the last sortie was marked by the death of Morgan. At least for the British the annoying fire from the American schooners was stopped when they were 'cut out' in a daring raid on the 12th.

After carrying a captain's gig and five *bateaux* 32km overland, 75 seamen and Royal Marines aided by the Lincoln militia then cut 12km of trail through woods to Lake Erie. After dark on 12 August they rowed in silence towards the American schooners and, when challenged, claimed they were provisioners. But once close in they had to fight, capturing *Somers* and *Ohio* although *Porcupine* managed to cut her cable and drift away. The British lost two dead and four wounded against one American killed and seven wounded. The following day the British siege battery opened fire, but the range was immediately found to be too great; William Dunlop noted in disgust that barely one shot in ten reached the ramparts and those that did rebounded like tennis balls.

ASSAULT

A singularly ineffective bombardment was carried on for two days before Drummond decided to attack, a consideration reinforced by his serious underestimation of the strength of the garrison. His plan was for an elaborate night assault by three converging columns: one against Snake Hill and two from the battery towards the north side of the fort itself, due to commence at 2am on 15 August. The largest column under Lieutenant-Colonel Victor Fischer consisted of 1,300 men from 1st/8th Regiment and Régiment de Watteville, the light companies of the 2nd/89th and 100th regiments plus some dragoons; it was to attack Snake Hill with fixed bayonets, but not only were muskets to be unloaded but their flints were to be removed.

This was partly to ensure that a negligent discharge did not reveal their roundabout approach, but it was also designed to force the troops 'to use the Bayonet with the effect which that valuable weapon has been ever found to possess in the hands of British soldiers', although William Dunlop for one was distinctly unimpressed by such tactics: 'In the British Army one would suppose that the only use of a musket was understood to be that it would carry a bayonet at the end of it.' A diversionary attack by Indians was to be made in the centre of the perimeter while two columns would attack in the north; one under Lieutenant-Colonel William Drummond of the 104th Regiment – to whom 'something whispered that this would be his last day' – where some 350 sailors, Royal Marines and light infantry would attack the small stone fort, and another on the far left with 700 men under Lieutenant-Colonel Hercules Scott of the 103rd Regiment would attack the entrenchments running from the fort to the lake shore.

However, the American garrison inside the perimeter had by now been reinforced with elements of the 9th, 11th, 17th, 19th, 21st, 22nd and 23rd US infantry, and New York and Pennsylvania militia supported by some dozen 6-pdrs, two 12-pdrs an 18-pdr and a 24-pdr, all reasonably well entrenched and protected by abatis – man-made obstacles of felled trees with their tangled, sharpened branches pointing outwards – while in all directions the approach to the position was a level open area cleared of vegetation, giving a clear field of observation and fire of 270–365m. Already expecting an attack when British rocket fire began on 14 August, Gaines decided an attack was imminent, and at about 4pm a mortar shell struck a small US magazine making a spectacular explosion. Despite causing little real damage it persuaded Drummond the bombardment was more effective than was really the case. Then, at about 12.30am the following morning, British fire slackened and ceased entirely an hour later, effectively alerting the Americans to impending assault.

From the beginning things went wrong when the Indians failed to make their scheduled demonstration; after struggling through the woods Fischer's column was then 30 minutes late getting into position and the forlorn hope comprising the Régiment de Watteville and part of the 1st/8th Regiment's light companies tripped an American picket bringing heavy fire down upon them. The main body could not then penetrate the abatis between the hill and the lake, discovering to their disgust that their five-metre scaling ladders were three metres too short. The result was that the Americans, 'finding only cheers to oppose them, got on top of the parapet and shot the unarmed men … like so many sheep'. They fell back in confusion under heavy fire without ever penetrating the American position. A few men tried a flanking movement by wading through the shallows of the lake but these were captured and the remainder fled.

Drummond's overcomplicated plan meant that Fischer had been driven off before the two columns attacking the north side of the fort could launch their assault; yet marching forwards to the sound of Fischer's battle they seemingly met with initial success, being fortunate that most of the American artillery fire went high. The left-hand column under Hercules Scott was first repulsed from the shore battery, then as Scott gathered the 103rd for the final charge it came under heavy and sustained musketry. Scott was mortally wounded then his second in command, Major William Smelt, was severely wounded; the 103rd recoiled and fell back in disorder.

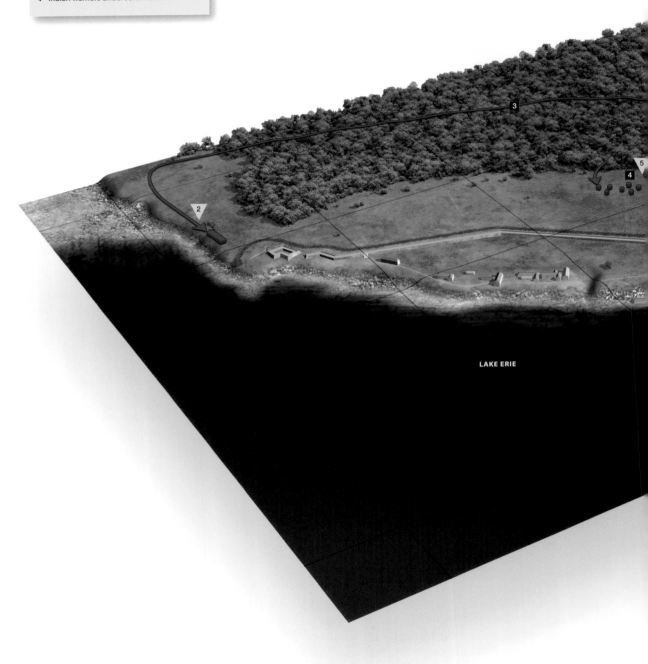

Note: Gridlines are shown at intervals of 250yds/228m

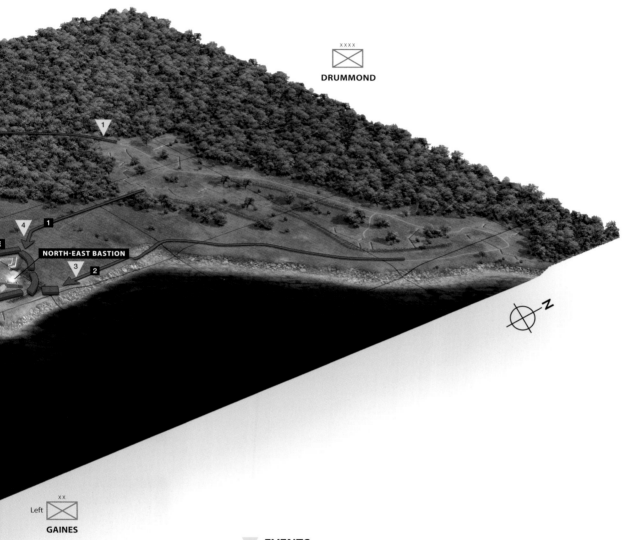

DRUMMOND

NORTH-EAST BASTION

Left GAINES

▼ **EVENTS**

1 At about 4pm Lt. Col. Victor Fischer's column sets out to reach its assault position, but poor weather, boggy conditions and dense undergrowth slows their progress, and they are not in position to launch the assault until 2am, considerably behind schedule.

2 When the British column trips an American picket the defences open a sustained fire that in 20 minutes defeats the British forlorn hope, including an attempt to outflank the abatis by wading chest-deep through the water. The main body's scaling ladders are too short, and unable to return fire they are soon chased off by the triumphant Americans.

3 The attack on Snake Hill is over by the time the British left-hand column appears at 3am. Alerted by the crunch of gravel along the shore, the Americans drive off two

gallant attempts to rush the abatis, killing Lt. Col. Hercules Scott and about one-third of his men. The column withdraws in confusion.

4 After two failed attempts, Lt. Col. William Drummond's column manages to wrest the north-east corner of Fort Erie from its defenders. But success at Snake Hill enables the Americans to rush up reinforcements before an almighty explosion in the magazine below the bastion destroys all hopes for British success.

5 The original plan called for a demonstration by the Indian warriors under John Norton, but his instructions were so vague that by the time he arrives on the scene he is only in time to witness the explosion and assist the dazed survivors back to their lines.

ASSAULT ON FORT ERIE, 15 AUGUST 1814

The British attempt to storm the fortifications of Fort Erie in the face of stern resistance form the American Left Division under their replacement commander Brigadier-General Edmund P. Gaines.

Led by the sailors the centre column under Lieutenant-Colonel Drummond was able to get through the abatis and into the ditch in front of the earth and wood curtain wall between the two demi-bastions of the fort. They placed their ladders, which were fortunately long enough, and climbed up as the Americans lunged at them with bayonets or the steel butt plates of their muskets, while gunners in the demi-bastions depressed their pieces as low as possible and fired canister. Having bloodily repulsed the British, American gunners under the command of Captain Alexander J. Williams 'instantly mounted our parapet and rent the air with loud huzzas, calling upon our brave foe to try it again'. The British did, twice more, then fell back to the ditch where they met remnants of the 103rd Regiment moving west, and the two columns mingled in an apparent blind spot in the defences.

Suddenly, up went the ladders and 2nd Lieutenant John Watmough, directing a gun, was startled as 'a British officer followed by several seamen and five or six soldiers jumped into the Bastion ...' He recognized the colonel from his appearance at the fort under a flag of truce, as Drummond lunged at Watmough with his boarding-pike which the American avoided; more British poured in from different sides, and Watmough remembered 'the enemy repeatedly called out on charging, to "surrender" – called us "dam'd Yankees" and even "rascals" I believe they called the men and repeated "no quarter, no quarter".' But Watmough survived as he 'received the blow on my side that knocked me [off the bastion] over into the ditch'. The other officers in the position, Captain Williams and Lieutenant Patrick McDonough, were not so fortunate; they were killed, as were those gunners who did not flee.

Drummond and his men had gained the bastion, but the only way into the fort's interior was down a steep two-metre-wide flight of steps between the bastion and a stone mess building. The fort's commander, Major W. A. Trimble of the 19th US Infantry, reacted quickly and ordered Lieutenant John McIlwain to take men from the curtain wall and bring the passageway under fire. McIlwain reported that the 'enemy made two or three charges, three I think, to come out' but, by 'heavy fire and by some charges we drove them back', while American attempts to get into the bastion proved equally futile resulting in a stand-off. During one British charge Trimble pointed out to McIlwain 'an officer advanced as far as the door of the mess house ... [and] gave us orders to kill him – we shot him down and his party gave back at his fall.' William Drummond's premonition had come true, and with his death the attack lost all momentum.

It was sometime after 4am and the lightening sky revealed some 200–300 men packed into the small north-east demi-bastion. Trimble ordered a force of 50 men into the second storey of the adjacent mess building to bring them under fire; the Americans squeezed three to a window to shoot into the huddled mass crouching for cover. In between rounds, they taunted: 'Come over you rascals, we're British deserters and Irish rebels!' Those American guns that could cover the north-east corner of the fort also began to fire on them as, incredibly, some men were still trying to get up the ladders into the fort. But seeing the hopelessness of the situation, others 'were sneaking out by one, two or three from the ditch' for the cover of the British lines.

In desperation, Lieutenant George Charlton RA somehow traversed a 24-pdr gun in the bastion around, and fired 'once thro' the mess house', and a second time at American positions to the east. Then, as William Dunlop was 'scrambling over some dead bodies, an explosion took place. At first I thought it was a shell had burst close to me, for the noise was not greater if so great,

as that of a large shell; but the tremendous glare of light and falling of beams and rubbish soon demonstrated that it was something more serious.' It was probably the muzzle flash from Charlton's gun dropping sparks through the cracks in the bastion's wooden floor that ignited the magazine below, for suddenly, recalled American bombardier, Lieutenant David B. Douglass, 'every sound was hushed by the sense of an unnatural tremor, beneath our feet, like the first heave of an earthquake,' and then, 'the centre of the bastion burst up, with a terrific explosion; and a jet of flame, mingled with the fragments of timber, earth, stone, and bodies of men, rose, to the height of one or two hundred feet in the air, and fell, in a shower of ruins, to a great distance all around.'

Lieutenant John Le Couteur had just mounted a scaling ladder and got over the palisade. Afterwards he remembered 'seeing a black volume rise from the earth and I lost my senses'. The colossal explosion enabled the Americans, now reinforced from Snake Hill, to drive the demoralized remnant of attackers out of the position, although an anonymous American witness later claimed the magazine detonation was detrimental to the Americans as 'it caused the precipitate retreat of [the British] reserve, which should have been intercepted in a few moments more, and in all probability made prisoners'. In fact Drummond appears to have made no attempt to reinforce the British lodgement with the reserve under the hapless Colonel Tucker; but whether true or not, the failure to secure the fort was a very severe setback, the most 'unfortunate business that happened [to] us during the war', according to William H. Merritt.

The British posted casualties of 59 dead including colonels Drummond and Scott, 309 wounded and no fewer than 539 missing, with the 103rd losing 424 men including 14 out of 18 officers, and the two flank companies of the 104th losing 54 out of 77 men engaged. Drummer Jarvis Hanks 'counted 196 bodies lying in the ditch and about the fort', and the youngster was transfixed by the sight of 'legs, arms and heads lying, in confusion, separated, by the concussions, from the trunks to which they had long been attached'. The explosion 'was tremendous', reported Gaines, 'it was decisive'. He later reported 222 dead British had been found on the position, while total

Surgeons at work, siege of Fort Erie. As one American recorded, the dead from the explosion were 'thrown out of the lower or east side of the Bastion' and 'principally lay in one pile …' The wounded from both sides were sent to a tented hospital at Williamsville near Buffalo. (Drawing by George Balbar, courtesy of Haunted Press)

American losses came to 84. Since Chippawa the British had lost 2,300 men for no tangible gain and although Drummond tried to blame the failure on 'the present disgraceful, and unfortunate, conduct of the troops', and in particular the foreigners of the Régiment de Watteville, this cut little ice with Prevost or the authorities in London who were appalled by the losses and blamed poor leadership.

For the most part the men had fought bravely against a vigilant and valiant enemy, and it seems the blame lies more fairly on the plan of attack; an anonymous officer of the 41st Regiment damned the order to remove the flints from the muskets. 'Alas! If this absurd order had not been issued I have no sort of doubt that we should have carried the fortress.' Indeed, Drummond was an inexperienced commander who had never directed siege operations, and while the preliminary bombardment was clearly inadequate, surprise was also totally lacking. Fortunately for Drummond he now received some 1,200 reinforcements from Burlington and York, for his position languishing in front of Fort Erie was fundamentally weak: although he continued the siege, the American naval blockade on Lake Ontario against which he railed repeatedly ensured his men remained short of provisions, ammunition and equipment – especially tents – just as the weather turned cool and rainy.

Control of Lake Ontario would be the key to further campaigns if the war was to continue into 1815, and consequently the Royal Navy had built HMS *St Lawrence*, a behemoth of 102 guns (sometimes rated as 104 or even 112). Unfortunately the continued delay in launching the mighty ship, more powerful than Nelson's *Victory*, led Prevost to report to London on 27 August that 'all hopes of using our Squadron on Lake Ontario, before the first week in October have vanished'. Yet so grave a threat did this ship pose that Chauncey hired a renegade Canadian, Bill Johnson, to try and blow her up before she was launched. Though nothing came of this it would not have been a difficult task, as Captain R. E. Armstrong of the Nova Scotia Fencibles reported nervously that only six sentries guarded the ship. 'Notwithstanding I am convinced I could burn her with fifty determined fellows. We are of course very anxious to get her launched and out of our hands.'

The Americans by contrast took great heart from their successful defence of the fort, although for six weeks Lieutenant-Colonel Thomas Aspinwall of 9th US Infantry 'seldom got more than 3 or four hours daily repose, and never undressed or even pulled off my boots'. Both sides were plagued by supply shortages but things were probably worse for the British; on 18 August Drummond's commissary officer reported that food stocks were down to four weeks rather than the six to seven previously thought. Drummond desperately called for a company of sappers and miners, camp stores, food and tents and for Yeo's assistance; without tents the men lived in scrapes and shelters, poor protection from the appalling weather while the Americans grew increasingly aggressive. But on 28 August a shell crashed through the roof of Gaines's room badly wounding him, and although not fully recovered from his own injuries, Brown was forced to resume command.

Lieutenant Philpott constructed a second battery some 730m from the fort but this proved ineffective when it commenced firing on 29 August, forced as it was to conserve ammunition. Still Drummond urged Yeo to get out onto Lake Ontario and secure his position. Fortunately for the Americans, Drummond was reluctant to renew the assault without express instructions, and persistent heavy rain in early September further dampened his division's spirits and raised sickness levels, so that trenches 'filled with Water, & the chilling blasts of Autumn began to be felt'.

On 2 September Ripley and a council of officers came out in favour of evacuation but Brown would not accept this. His main difficulty was that the British had completed a third battery south-east of the second one and only 365m from the fort, well capable of causing immense damage. Furthermore, Drummond had amassed 200 rounds per gun, and with Major-General James Kempt's Brigade comprising the 9th (East Norfolk), 37th (North Hampshire) 57th (West Middlesex) and 81st regiments arriving at Kingston the local commander, Major-General Richard Stovin, was able to forward as reinforcements 1,200 men of the 6th and 82nd regiments – both Peninsula veteran units – while retaining the 97th Regiment until Drummond should call for them.

PLATTSBURGH

While matters developed on the Niagara Peninsula, to the east there was a brief flurry of activity as Prevost finally took advantage of the reinforcements that had arrived from Europe to launch his invasion of northern New York, although his objectives remained limited as his instructions were 'not to expose His Majesty's Forces to being cut off by too extended a line of advance'. Instead he was to gain a foothold on Lake Champlain sufficient to force its demilitarization at the peace conference. But his natural caution was, in any case, reinforced by the lack of naval strength.

In August, Armstrong ordered Brigadier-General George Izard to Sackets Harbor, which left Brigadier-General Alexander Macomb in command of forces around Lake Champlain, amounting to some 3,400 in total – of whom

Master-Commandant Thomas Macdonough, US Navy (1783–1825). Promoted to master-commandant on 24 July 1813, Macdonough prepared his fleet despite a lack of guns, stores and experienced sailors. But the British were even worse off, and forced to draft soldiers from the 39th Regiment to man their ships on Lake Champlain. (Library of Congress)

Macomb reported only some 1,500 were effectives – and leaving the entire region dangerously exposed. Born in Detroit in 1782, Macomb briefly served during the quasi-war with France until 1800 before he was commissioned into the Corps of Engineers in 1802, spending five years in charge of coastal fortifications in the Carolinas and Georgia. Now he was faced with overwhelming odds as for the proposed operation three British brigades were available: the 1st Brigade under Major-General Frederick Robinson comprised the 3rd/27th (Inniskilling), 39th (Dorsetshire), 76th and 88th (Connaught Rangers) regiments, the 2nd Brigade under Major-General Thomas Brisbane was drawn from troops already stationed in Lower Canada – 2nd/8th, 13th, 49th (Hertfordshire) regiments, the Swiss Régiment de Meuron and the Voltigeurs Canadiens – and Major-General Manley Power's 3rd Brigade comprising the 3rd (East Kent), 5th (Northumberland), 1st/27th and 58th regiments, each supported by a Royal Artillery brigade of five 6-pdrs and one 5½in. howitzer, together with 309 officers and men of the 19th Light Dragoons to give the division a total strength on paper of 10,351 regulars and militia.

Thus, they were not all Peninsula veterans as is sometimes assumed, and the figure does not take into account sick or personnel detached for one reason or another, so the actual invasion strength was lower. Besides, the Peninsula veterans were by no means happy soldiers. After almost six years continuous campaigning across burning plains and freezing mountains they had expected to return home; instead they had been separated from 'the poor faithful Spanish and Portuguese women, hundreds of whom had attached themselves to our soldiers, and who had accompanied them through all their fatigues and dangers, were from stern necessity obliged to be abandoned to their fate'.

Prevost had been disturbed all summer by Yeo's siphoning of manpower, naval stores and guns to Kingston for use on Lake Ontario, and shortage of crew hampered the development of HMS *Confiance* (36) – named after the French ship Yeo had captured much earlier in his career. She was launched on 25 August but was far from combat ready, and her impact was reduced by news that the Americans had launched *Eagle* (20) ten days earlier. *Confiance* carried 27 long 24-pdrs and six carronades which would enable her to defeat the American *Saratoga* (eight long 24s and 18 larger carronades) at long range, while the other vessels in the rival squadrons were roughly equal and cancelled each other out. However, hopes of naval efficiency were not helped by changes in senior personnel. Captain Peter Fisher RN had arrived to take command on Lake Champlain on 24 June with Commander Daniel Pring RN as his deputy, but, on 2 September, Fisher was summarily replaced by Captain George Downie RN, despite being the more experienced officer. Fisher's brief tenure and abrupt replacement only disrupted the Royal Navy's preparations.

Command within the army was no more harmonious; Prevost chose to quibble over dress regulations with the generals newly arrived from Europe, complaining about 'a fanciful variety inconsistent with the rules of service' to veteran officers who knew better, and unsurprisingly such fusty orders provoked resentment, and went a long way to damage the army's confidence in Prevost. Fortunately for the United States, Prevost also decided that now was a good time to take the field personally, and he soon found himself in conflict with his experienced brigade commanders who resented being told the minutiae of campaign management by a man they regarded as little more than a pen-pusher. It would have been far better for all concerned had one of these officers been appointed commander of the expedition for, as Robinson

later wrote in his journal, the army moved without a clear plan and made no effort to gather intelligence; Prevost apparently believed that 'it was throwing money away to attempt it'.

Robinson's distrust of Prevost's ability and judgement was significant, as the experienced Robinson was highly rated by the Duke of Wellington having served in England, Ireland and the West Indies before arriving in the Peninsula in 1812 as a brigadier-general, and being promoted the following year. On 1 September – the day Downie arrived to take up his command – the army crossed the frontier. The timing was certainly inauspicious; the following morning Downie ordered Pring to take the dozen or so gunboats of his flotilla out in support of the army, and the same day Master-Commandant Thomas Macdonough USN, commanding the American Lake Champlain squadron, brought his three warships and supporting gunboats into Plattsburgh Bay. Born in New Castle County, Delaware (modern MacDonough), young Thomas had enlisted in the navy in 1800 and served with distinction on the *Constellation* during the Barbary War. In 1812 he was commanding gunboats defending Portland before being re-assigned as commander of naval forces in Lake Champlain in October.

The British made slow progress along appalling roads reaching Beekmantown Corners on the 5th, some 13km from Plattsburgh, where they camped on the farm of Miner Lewis. Faced by overwhelming odds the Americans retired across the river and took up the bridges and, 'except [for] a brave men, fell back most precipitately in the greatest disorder, notwithstanding the British troops did not deign to fire on them, except by their flankers and advanced patrols. … So undaunted was the [British force], that he never deployed in his whole march, always pressing on in column.'

Early on the morning of 6 September the British advanced in two columns; the left-hand column under Brisbane took the Lake Road and the right-hand column under Power followed the Beekmantown Road, driving some American militia and 250 regulars before it and turning Macomb's position at the Deer Creek Bridge on the lake road where he had abatis manned by riflemen. Initially some militia rallied to their support, but dissolved into

Major-General Frederick Philipse Robinson, British Army (1763–1852). The fourth son of an American loyalist, young Frederick received an ensigncy in 1777. When the peace of 1783 destroyed the loyalists' hopes Robinson had to make a career in the army. (Painting by George Theodore Berthon, c.1884, Government of Ontario Art Collection, Archives of Ontario.)

flight when some New York dragoons wearing red coats appeared behind them – ironically, British light dragoons wore dark blue jackets – and this forced Macomb to retreat. At Beekmantown Lieutenant-Colonel James Wellington and Ensign J. Chapman of the 3rd Regiment were killed by a sniper, Samuel Terry of Peru, Clinton County, New York, and the Americans retired across the river and took up the bridges. The British reached Plattsburgh that evening.

Prevost asked Robinson if he could attack immediately, but Robinson indicated that his men had been marching all day without food, and the fords across the river had yet to be identified. He also wanted naval support from the lake against the American fortifications and the American lake squadron which was anchored offshore. Prevost had always maintained that naval control of the lake was essential and on the morning of 7 September wrote to Downie, some 24km away, giving details of the American squadron and requesting that if Downie deemed it possible, it be dealt with; he also stated that his own actions were dependent on Downie's decision, and berated Downie for not getting into position sooner.

Downie replied that he would engage as soon as *Confiance* was ready, but that this would take a day or two, to which Prevost replied he urgently needed the fleet's support and that he was waiting for it; he sent further letters seemingly designed to rush the much younger and junior Downie into action. But as Downie pointed out, his duty was not to commit his forces before they were ready, and he would have to defeat the American squadron consisting of the ship *Saratoga* (26), brig *Eagle* (20), schooner *Ticonderoga* (17), sloop *Preble* (7) and ten gunboats with a total manpower of almost 900. Against this he deployed *Confiance*, the brig *Linnet* (16), sloops *Chubb* (11) and *Finch* (10), and 11 gunboats. Prevost's claims that American deserters were reporting their squadron as inefficiently manned did not reassure Downie who had to use a company of the 39th Regiment to supplement his few sailors. Thus, while the two fleets were broadly equal in numbers and firepower, the British were clearly inferior in manpower. Not until the evening of 9 September did Downie write to say he would enter Plattsburgh Bay the following day, but then he was held up by contrary winds.

On the morning of the 11th Downie wrote to say he would be arriving and Prevost planned to launch his assault simultaneously. Plattsburgh was divided by the Saranac River and the Americans had three strong redoubts and two blockhouses to the south of it crossing the neck of a small peninsula between the river and the lake. Covered by fire from the new batteries, Brisbane's Brigade would make a diversionary attack at the two stripped plank bridges while Robinson led a force comprising his own 3rd/27th and 76th regiments with Power's Brigade and the light companies of the 39th and 88th regiments, two squadrons of 19th Light Dragoons and an artillery detachment of two 6-pdrs and Congreve rockets – to a ford further up the Saranac to cross the river and assault the American works with scaling ladders. Robinson's force waited from an hour before dawn but was told by Prevost not to march off before 10am; as Robinson went to Prevost's headquarters to receive his final orders he heard Downie's guns in action.

Under pressure from Prevost, Downie tried to sail into the bay in a light and variable breeze and place *Confiance* alongside Macdonough on *Saratoga*, but he was unable to get closer than about 275m. *Saratoga* waited until she was anchored to return fire and then, with her guns double-shotted, she delivered a destructive broadside. *Linnet* anchored to engage *Eagle* aided by

Battle of Plattsburgh, 9 September 1814

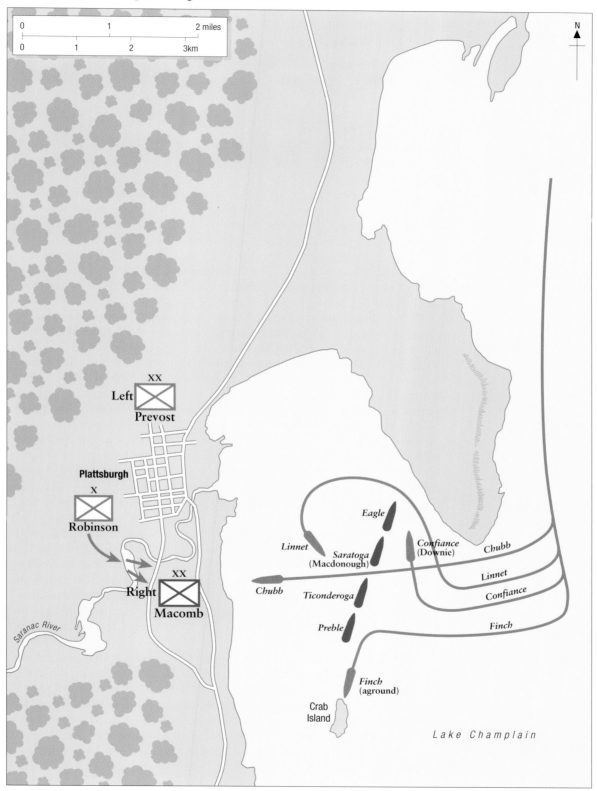

Battle of Plattsburgh. Robinson soon had four battalions across and was ready to launch his final assault, one that appeared straightforward compared with any against the French, when he received the order to retire. The feeling that success was at hand, at least on land, only added to British disappointment. (Lossing's *Pictorial Field Book*)

Chubb, while *Finch* and most of the British gunboats took on *Ticonderoga*, *Preble* and the American gunboats. But the battle soon turned against the British; after just 15 minutes Downie was cut down and killed by a gun knocked loose from a carriage, and the two British sloops were lost with *Finch* being disabled and drifting onto Crab Island, where she came under fire from a shore battery manned by American sick. *Chubb* also drifted out of control and was taken by a midshipman from *Saratoga* and the only British success was the forcing inshore of *Preble* by gunboats.

By 10.30am it was clear that all British hopes now rested on the *Confiance* carrying the day; *Eagle* had been under fire from both *Linnet* and *Confiance* and had the springs of her cable shot away. Her captain cut the cable and anchored between *Confiance* and *Ticonderoga*, which left *Saratoga* exposed to fire from Linnet. 'Although the bombs were bursting in all directions,' wrote American seaman Jonathan Stevens later, 'they seemed as harmless as tho' it was only a game at ball or some amusement.' Both *Confiance* and *Saratoga* suffered dreadfully with Macdonough's starboard battery in no state to reply, but at this point Macdonough's seamanship saved the day. He managed to wind his ship round on an anchor and hawsers to bring his larboard battery to bear, stuffed to the muzzle with hand spikes, into the throng of British sailors trying to turn the *Confiance*. 'Where it had been black with men the moment before, scarcely one man could now be seen', noted Seaman Asa Fitch.

Lieutenant James Robertson RN, who had taken over from Downie, recalled that having received 105 shot through her hull, 'the Ship's Company declared they would no longer stand to their Quarters, nor could their officers with their utmost exertions rally them', and *Confiance* was forced to strike her colours. *Saratoga* then sprung round to engage *Linnet* and she too struck 15 minutes later. The British gunboats then fled, leaving Macdonough with a famous victory that cost 52 killed and 58 wounded to British losses of 80 killed and 100 wounded.

As soon as the British squadron appeared Prevost ordered his land assault to begin, but the guides for Robinson's column took the wrong road causing a one-hour delay. They then rushed the shallow ford that was defended by American volunteers and militia while the regulars defended the bridge site, Robinson reported, dashing 'down a very steep and high bank and forded the river like so many fox hounds driving the Doodles before them'. Just as he was preparing to exploit this initial success Robinson received an order from Prevost to retire; it took him completely by surprise, and Power was 'equally astonished'. But as soon as Prevost realized the naval squadron had been beaten he had cancelled the entire operation, and had it not been for the hour's delay it is likely that the British would have already secured victory on the ground.

Instead, Robinson's men had to retire losing three officers and 31 men of the Light Company of the 76th Regiment who, out in front, failed to receive word to do so. The Régiment de Meuron watched the battle from Plattsburgh, recalled Lieutenant Charles de Goumoëns. The regiment 'was supposed to mount its own attack during the naval combat. But the order was never given by General Prevost who thus committed a grave error as the Swiss could have taken the Fort and from there bombard the American fleet, and thus prevent them from occupying the grounded British fleet …' Yeo later insisted that Prevost's urging of Downie to attack an American squadron in an anchorage of its own choosing put the junior man at a grave disadvantage; had Prevost stormed the American position the American squadron would have been forced to put out into the lake where the British could meet it on equal terms.

Brigadier-General Alexander Macomb, US Army (1782–1841). Thanks to rivalry between Gaines and Scott, Macomb was appointed Commanding General of the Army from 1828 to 1841. This oil on canvas painting was made by Thomas Sully (1783–1872) in 1829. (West Point Museum Art Collection, United States Military Academy, West Point, New York)

Certainly, Prevost achieved greater celerity in retreat than he did in the advance. That evening the baggage was sent to the rear and the batteries dismantled, and before daylight the following day the troops were marching back to Canada having destroyed excess ammunition and stores. American losses on the ground were 38 killed, 64 wounded and 20 missing. Officially British losses were 37 dead, 150 wounded and 55 missing, although many more took the opportunity to desert. On 15 September Macomb reported over 300 had already come in with more arriving daily, disgusted by the retreat and tempted by American offers of high pay.

Pring reached the British lines on 16 September under his parole and represented Macdonough as being 'most delicate, honorable and kind. Thus [the Americans] are making themselves respected by their generosity of character, as well as their gallantry.' But Prevost tried to place the blame for defeat entirely on the naval action. Certainly it is true that once the lake was lost he had little option but to withdraw, as he could not rely on tenuous road communications that could easily have been cut now control of the lake was lost. Yet it is difficult to resist the conclusion that a more confident and aggressive commander would have quickly overrun Macomb's small force and forced the American squadron out of Plattsburgh Bay, either to confront the British in open waters or even to seek refuge elsewhere. Despite victory really belonging to Macdonough's sailors, Macomb converted his own fortunate escape into a military victory, and was styled 'The Hero of Plattsburgh' by the American press. He was promoted major-general and received the thanks of Congress and a Congressional Gold Medal.

As Captain J. H. Wood RA later noted, the 'unnecessary precipitancy of our retreat, or more properly speaking, our *flight* … is spoken of with disgust and indignation'. But Prevost was not a commander to take risks, and a sudden abundance of experienced troops could not transform him into a dynamic and effective field commander. Yeo did not agree that the naval battle was 'unlooked for', as Prevost claimed, and became convinced that Prevost had hurried Downie into a doomed venture. In due course he would lay charges, but even before Plattsburgh angry civilians were sending vicious reports about Prevost back to London, such as Alicia Cockburn who claimed had 'any man with common abilities been at the head of this Government … we must long ago have taught the Yankees submission, & been at Peace'. The Prime Minister, Lord Liverpool, decided that the army had lost confidence in him and relieved Prevost of command.

MÊLÉE AROUND THE BRITISH BATTERIES, 17 SEPTEMBER

Although Brown later estimated the entire sortie against the British siege lines lasted only about an hour from start to finish, a soldier of the 21st US Infantry described it as a savage encounter where 'man to man and steel to steel, across carriages and at the mouth of the guns, every inch of ground was disputed, and both American and Briton fell to mingle in one common dust'. Following the first rush the Americans in the second battery became disorganized and only too late did they realize redcoats were approaching them through the forest. As they desperately tried to form a line, the 6th and 82nd regiments closed and delivered several shattering volleys into the confused mass, following which they charged with the bayonet and quickly retook the battery. The British continued out of the forest and into the clearing outside the fort where the Americans rallied behind a small ravine, but after a hot fight and several more volleys from the redcoats, they retired into the

fort. The 82nd then moved out of range of the fort's guns engaging the British infantry and the battle dissolved into scattered shooting. It represented Porter's finest hour as a soldier, and he subsequently received a gold medal under a joint resolution of Congress dated 3 November 1814 'for gallantry and good conduct' during the campaign. He later served briefly as Secretary of War to President John Quincy Adams and died at Niagara Falls in 1844.

Within the trenches of the siege battery, surrounded by woods, and lined with wooden supports **(1)**, American troops **(2)** are intermingled in a bayonet fight with British of the 82nd Regiment **(3)** who are counterattacking them. Some of the Americans are militia wearing civilian clothes but with red cloth bands tied around their hats and arms **(4)**.

SORTIE

Meanwhile at Fort Erie artillery fire was exchanged daily as skirmishing continued, though it served little purpose. But on 4 September, Porter led a sortie to attack the second battery that saw six hours of fighting until a heavy downpour 'tended to cool both parties'. But during this fight Joseph Willcocks was shot in the chest and killed, which caused great rejoicing in the British lines. Despite this coup, however, Drummond felt overwhelmed with difficulties, and four days later warned Prevost of the 'possibility of my being compelled by sickness or suffering of the troops, exposed as they will be to the effects of the wet and unhealthy Season which is fast approaching, to withdraw them from their present Position to one which may afford them the means of cover. Sickness has, I am sorry to say, already made its appearance in several of the corps, particularly the 82nd.'

Although on 10 September Yeo finally launched *St Lawrence*, neither Drummond nor Prevost had much faith in the navy's ability to cooperate with land operations, intent as both sides now were on defeating the other's fleet. Drummond continued to complain of lack of ammunition and reinforcement as he lost heart, and on 15 September he restricted his guns to one round each per hour. The following day his new second in command, Major-General Louis de Watteville, urged him to abandon the siege and withdraw, which he seems to have accepted. But just as the batteries were starting to pack up on 17 September, suddenly the Americans came boiling out of the fort to attack them.

RIGHT
Régiment de Meuron. Raised by the French in 1781 the Régiment de Meuron served the Dutch East India Company before entering British service in 1795. It fought in the Mysore campaign of 1799, and then served in England, Gibraltar and Malta before leaving in May 1813 to serve in Canada. (Parks Canada)

LEFT
By 1815 Prevost's cautious nature was already the subject of ridicule and a vicious whispering campaign. He returned to Britain in early 1815 but died a year later, before having the chance to clear his name at court martial. (Toronto Public Library, T-15460)

LEFT

Soldier, Battalion Company, 6th (1st Warwickshire) Regiment of Foot. Raised in 1674, the 6th (1st Warwickshire) Regiment served in Portugal and Spain in 1808–09. During the Walcheren Expedition it was nearly destroyed by sickness, leaving only 93 men fit for duty. Consequently, 1810–12 saw the 6th serving in England and Ireland. (Courtesy, Royal Regiment of Fusiliers Museum, Warwick)

RIGHT

Officer, Light Company, 6th (1st Warwickshire) Regiment of Foot. The 6th returned to Spain in November 1812, fighting at Vittoria and Orthez. After Bonaparte's defeat in April 1814, reinforcements including the 6th and 82nd (Prince of Wales' Volunteers) regiments were sent to Canada, many being Peninsula veterans. (Courtesy, Royal Regiment of Fusiliers Museum, Warwick)

Having first set up his command post at Buffalo with Ripley in charge of the fort, Brown crossed over at the behest of his senior officers who had no confidence in Ripley. Finding the garrison 'impatient', he then decided to attack the No. 3 Battery and was encouraged by the improved response of the militia; 1,500 men had now volunteered to cross into Canada under Porter. To this raid Brown committed 2,000 men against one brigade of British in the siege lines, hoping to be away again before they could bring up reserves from their main camp. Inexplicably Drummond took no precautions despite warnings from American deserters that a raid was in the offing. His engineers left standing the dense woods that were within pistol shot of No. 3 Battery, and all through 16 September American fatigue parties were able to open a path to this point.

At midday, in heavy rain that masked their movement and lulled the British sentries, Porter led 1,600 regulars and militia through the woods running from Snake Hill to outflank the British position on the extreme right of the line to No. 3 Battery, and caught them unprepared. The battery was taken almost immediately, the guns spiked and the magazine blown up. Now covered by a

82

Porter's sortie from Fort Erie, 17 September 1814

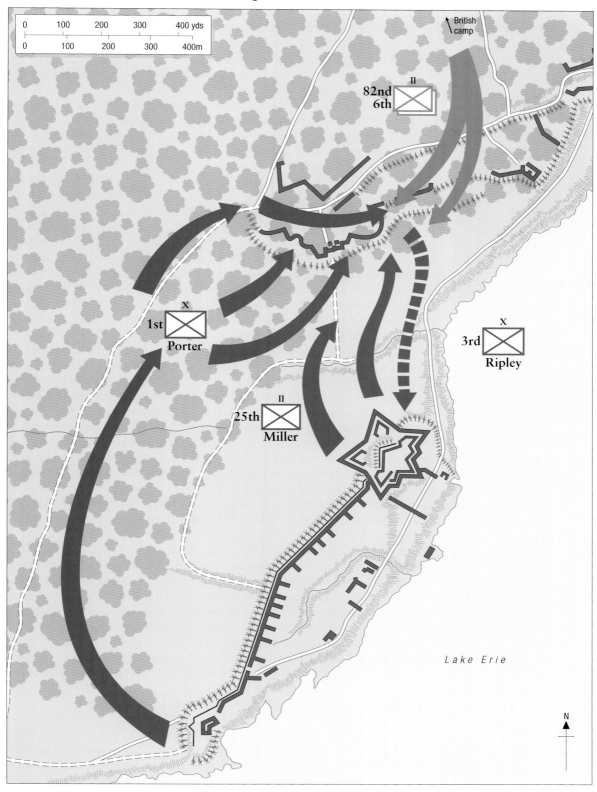

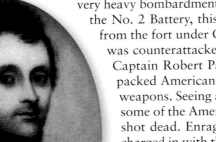

Major Sackville Brownlow Taylor, 6th (1st Warwickshire) Regiment of Foot. 'The brilliant style in which the battery No. 2 was recovered … by seven companies of the Eighty-second, under the command of Major Proctor, and three companies of the Sixth Regiment, detached under Major [Sackville Brownlow] Taylor [shown here], excited Lieut.-General Drummond's admiration, and entitle these troops to his particular thanks.'(Courtesy, Royal Regiment of Fusiliers Museum, Warwick)

very heavy bombardment from the fort itself the column moved on to attack the No. 2 Battery, this time aided by a column of 400 regulars sallying from the fort under Colonel James Miller. At this stage Porter's column was counterattacked by two companies of the 82nd Regiment under Captain Robert Patteson, who poured a concentrated fire into the packed American ranks so tightly crowded that few could use their weapons. Seeing an officer, Patteson demanded his surrender, but as some of the Americans began to ground their muskets Patteson was shot dead. Enraged at this apparently dishonourable act, his men charged in with the bayonet and slaughtered many Americans as the fighting became general, and Porter and Miller began to lose control as their commands intermingled.

The No. 2 Battery fell only after very heavy fighting where the British were protected by trenches, so that 'constant use of the bayonet was the only mode of assailing them', recalled Private Jesse P. Harmon; and by now the British reserves had arrived. These included seven more companies of the 82nd and three of the 6th Regiment under Major Henry Adolphus Proctor of the 82nd, who made a fine charge to drive the Americans back. Seeing that things were not going entirely well Brown sent Ripley forwards with the reserve, but Ripley lost his way in the tangled undergrowth and was badly wounded. More fighting took place around No. 1 Battery before the Americans retired, harassed by Indians and the Glengarry Light Infantry.

With Drummond already committed to retiring the Americans lost 72 killed – including their invaluable engineer officer, Eleazar D. Wood – with 432 wounded and missing in what was essentially an unnecessary operation, although Brown could not have known that; British losses were 115 killed, 178 wounded and 316 missing, over half coming from the 1st/8th and Régiment de Watteville who had been in the forward lines, and were taken completely by surprise in the initial American assault. For despite the fierce nature of the later fighting Private Eber D. Howe, an American who encountered the Swiss mercenaries, noted: 'Many of them threw away their arms and in their attempts to run would fling themselves full length upon the ground, quite willing and anxious to be prisoners.' Furthermore, three of Drummond's six siege guns were now disabled and their ammunition had been destroyed.

Ignoring his own errors Drummond now wrote to Prevost that 'the sickness of the troops has increased to such an alarming degree, and their situation has really become one of such extreme wretchedness from the torrents of rain which have continued to fall for the last 13 days, and from the circumstance of the Division being entirely destitute of camp equipage, that I feel it my duty no longer to persevere in a vain attempt to maintain the blockade …' The British buried the dead of both sides and, further delayed by rain, finally pulled out of their lines on 21 September to retreat towards Chippawa as the summer campaign season finally drew to a miserable close.

COOK'S MILLS AND MALCOLM'S MILLS

For his part Brown was waiting for Izard's reinforcements to arrive from Plattsburgh; they completed their arduous trek on 12 October, the combined force now totalling some 7,000. The more aggressive Brown wished to attack Drummond immediately, but Izard chose not to risk casualties by attacking a strong defensive position. Angered at Izard's inaction and with the Royal Navy now controlling Lake Ontario, Brown marched his division back to protect Sackets Harbor; and seeing no purpose in retaining Fort Erie except as a trophy, he prepared it for demolition. Despite Brown's departure Drummond dug in his now heavily outnumbered and battle-weary survivors behind Chippawa Creek in preparation for a renewed American assault. Izard, however, refused to attack frontally such strong positions, but eventually decided on a plan to lure Drummond away from his defensive position.

Intelligence indicated a quantity of grain was stored at Cook's Mills on Lyons Creek, a tributary of the Chippawa, so Izard sent a brigade under Brigadier-General Daniel Bissell with about 1,200 men to capture it. On 18 October, skirmishing between his riflemen and a detachment of Glengarry Light Infantry led Bissell to believe a sizeable British force was opposing him across the creek. In fact, Drummond had sent about 750 men under Lieutenant-Colonel Christopher Myers of the 100th Regiment to protect Cook's Mills, which Lieutenant John Le Couteur recalled involved 'marching 'knee deep in mud in a pitch dark night – over rough and smooth – an exquisite enjoyment for those who have never tried it'.

On the morning of the 19 October, Myers attacked and drove the lead American units back across Lyon's Creek. The British crossed the creek but Bissell managed to hold them off and immediately planned a counterattack. The Americans surged across the creek and Myers retreated in orderly fashion, losing one man dead and 35 wounded to 12 Americans killed and 54 wounded. The Americans then took Cook's Mills and burned about 200 bushels of wheat. Despite this success it became apparent that Drummond was not going to move from his defences, so Izard withdrew back to Fort Erie.

Meanwhile, starting on 22 October an American force of about 700 Kentucky and Ohio riflemen, 75 Wyandot warriors, 50 Rangers and a few militia under Brigadier-General Duncan McArthur launched a raid into western Upper Canada aimed at the British reserve position at Burlington Heights. McArthur made his way undetected as far as Moraviantown which

HMS *St Lawrence*. An unknown artist captured HMS *St Lawrence* as she stood on the stocks at Point Frederick where crowds of people from Kingston and surrounding villages gathered to watch what must have been a great sensation. Her first cruise was made on 16 October, but she was never to see action. (Royal Ontario Museum, 74 CAN 258.967.106.1)

McArthur's raid into south-western Upper Canada, October–November 1814

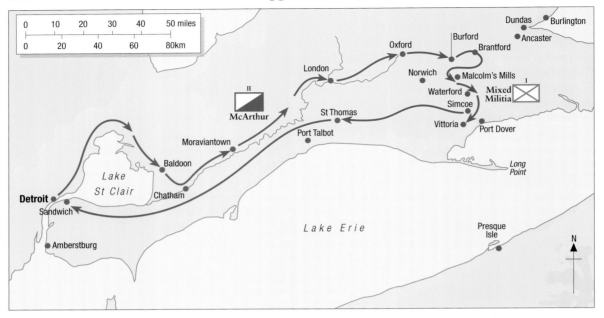

he reached on 30 October, then advanced rapidly along the Thames. He intended to devastate the Thames and Grand River settlements and the region around the head of Lake Ontario which supplied British forces on the Niagara Frontier, and during his aggressive march to Oxford County, the Americans burned houses, barns and mills, reaching Oxford itself on 4 November. The Oxford militia commander, Lieutenant-Colonel Henry Bostwick, decided to join with the Norfolk militia to defend the Grand River area, but a traitor informed McArthur about the Canadian plan so he decided to move his men across the Grand River through Norfolk County to Lake Erie.

McArthur reached the Grand River and after an unsuccessful attempt to force a crossing, attacked a body of some 150 Canadians comprising elements of the 1st and 2nd Norfolk, 1st Oxford and 1st Middlesex regiments of militia, at Malcolm's Mills (modern Oakland) on 6 November. The Canadians put up a brief resistance but when they were outflanked they quickly withdrew, having lost two dead and three wounded to one American killed and six wounded. The Americans continued their foray, but apart from the destruction of five mills and the seizure of some 400 head of livestock the raid was of no wider significance, and they returned to Detroit on 17 November. The day before the action at Malcolm's Mills, Izard had blown up Fort Erie in a pyrotechnic display worthy of Guy Fawkes Night, then retired to the American shore.

Drummond returned to the remains of Fort Erie but chose not to rebuild it, and merely added makeshift quarters; it was eventually abandoned completely in 1821. Many American officers were disappointed by the way the campaign had fizzled out, and accused Izard of cowardice for which he was nearly court-martialled. But this hardest fought and bloodiest period of the war was well summed up by Surgeon William E. Horner: '[T]here was never a campaign in which the belligerents came to a better understanding of what they might expect in battle at each other's hands; and where leaders, though under the excitement of a state of war, left with more military respect for one another.'

Certainly the US Army had finally made up for the failures of 1812 and 1813, and had earned the respect of British troops, although in strategic terms they had been little more successful than previously. Drummond blamed a lack of men and supplies for his operational failures, but his own lack of drive, especially in the aftermath of Lundy's Lane, was at least as much to blame for British disappointments that year. Nevertheless, despite Prevost's failure to seize control of the area west of Lake Champlain the Niagara campaign overall represented strategic success for the British: the final US attempt to invade Canada had failed, and not a foot of British territory remained under American control.

AFTERMATH

Besides guaranteeing the integrity of British territory the Niagara campaign had no significant effects, for the war had been drawing to a close for some time. Negotiations for peace started at Ghent in the Netherlands during the summer, and the failure of British forces to secure victory at Baltimore or Plattsburgh became, by late 1814, sufficient inducement for Britain to settle terms. By 1814 Britain had been at war for 21 years and in concluding the war the Prime Minister, Lord Liverpool, was taking into account domestic opposition to continued taxation – especially among merchants keen to get back to doing business with America – and, more importantly, foreign policy considerations of much greater significance. The Foreign Secretary, Lord Castlereagh, had far more important matters to attend to; the Congress of Vienna would decide the future of Europe now that Bonaparte was defeated, and the prospect of the American War dragging on was an unnecessary distraction to be avoided, the wisdom of which course was amply justified with Bonaparte's escape from Elba the following spring.

During the autumn there was some talk in Government circles of sending the Duke of Wellington to America, but had he gone it would have been to preside over a diplomatic settlement, not to wage war. It is also worth

Signing of the Treaty of Ghent. This painting by A. Forrestier from 1915 is entitled *A Hundred Years of Peace*. The War of 1812 did not immediately produce good relations between Britain and the US, but it did pave the way for the 'Era of Good Feelings' in the latter. (Library and Archives Canada, C-5996)

Peace of Ghent 1814.

Minerva, represents the wisdom of the United States, Mercury their commerce; Hercules their force. Minerva, dictates the conditions of peace, which Mercury presents to Britannia and Hercules forces her to accept, on the shield of Minerva are the names of those who signed the Treaty, on the blockets those of the braves.

UNDER THE PRESIDENCE OF MADISSON MONROE SEC.RETARY OF STATE

Published by P.Price de Philada.

and Triumph of America

on the other side. America figures in Triumph through the Arch, in her way to the temple of peace attended by Victory and followed by a numerous train ... Trophies are seen and in the back ground are ... ruins of the Capitol.

considering that had he accepted the post he could not have been at Waterloo. But British possession of Fort Niagara, northern Maine and a vast swathe of Michigan territory was entirely unacceptable to the America delegation and, with a diplomatic rift now opening between Britain and Russia, Castlereagh was happy to forego territorial gain and accept the *status quo ante bellum* as the basis of peace, a position he had been advocating since the very beginning of the war.

For America the prospects were now bleak: she was practically bankrupt with no likelihood of respite; the entire Royal Navy was free to blockade her coast and the British Army to intervene in ever larger numbers which, despite its improved performance, the still tiny US Army could not hope to match. A treaty was duly signed on 24 December 1814, known as the Treaty of Ghent, or the Peace of Christmas Eve. However, peace was not easily declared in the days before the telegraph, and the news took weeks to cross the Atlantic enabling America's crushing victory at New Orleans to be fought on 8 January 1815. And since on three previous occasions America had insisted on modifications after her envoys had signed treaties, this time Britain insisted it could not become effective until both parties had ratified it, news of which did not reach London until 13 March, four days after Bonaparte's escape from Elba. This allowed troops due to go to America to deploy to Belgium instead, forming the basis of Wellington's victorious army at Waterloo.

Peace of Ghent and triumph of America. Although the USA had failed utterly to achieve any of her war aims as they stood in 1812, coming on the back of victories at Plattsburgh and New Orleans enabled Americans to turn the weary survival of 1814 into a 'glorious victory' in 1815. (Library of Congress, LC USZ62 - 3686)

Quartette from the new opera of the 'Whig celebration at Lundy's Lane'. Scott's performance at Lundy's Lane was turned to account by this artist during his bid for the White House, who shows Scott's abolitionist supporters hesitate to let Scott join the 'Whig Chorus', knowing his reputation for imprudent remarks. (Library of Congress, LC USZ 62 - 16010)

In the ensuing excitement the American War was quickly forgotten in Britain, while in the United States all that remained was for the post-war construction of a reassuring myth, which transformed Madison's futile and humiliating attempt to conquer Canada into one of defending the republic. The reception of the peace treaty in each country was determined by the timing of the news. The British public were disappointed after a period of heightened expectation of an important victory, while Americans could bask in the glow of New Orleans, and Republican papers like the Worcester *National Aegis*, simply ignored all other evidence and declared '*we have gloriously triumphed*!' Such claims were ridiculous even if, thanks to her effective commissioners, America might claim to have won the peace.

America had certainly enjoyed the more glamorous if less tangible successes, such as New Orleans and the early single-ship victories by the US Navy's frigates, and by publicizing these she turned weary survival into colourful victory, at least on the surface, while for decades afterwards successful participation in the war was worth thousands of votes to American politicians of every stripe, although they were insufficient to win the White House for Winfield Scott in 1852. For as the Niagara campaign demonstrated the war was really a failure for the United States, and although American military efforts eventually proved sufficient to sustain her diplomacy, this was only by discarding its basic tenets as they had stood in 1812.

THE BATTLEFIELDS TODAY

Chippawa battle site. The Niagara Parks Commission acquired the Chippawa battle site in 1995 and preserved 121 hectares of it. A self-guided walking tour shows the visitor the events of the battle while a memorial service is held every 5 July to commemorate the fallen of all the nations. (Author's collection)

The Niagara Peninsula is a thriving agricultural region with a number of large cities that all post-date the war, when the population of British North America was barely 500,000. But the authorities have taken some care over the years to preserve many of the sites that make it so important historically. Fortunately the town of Newark – now Niagara-on-the-Lake – retains the regency charm of its rebuilding after the war. On the other side of the Niagara River, Fort Niagara is probably the finest example of its type in all of North America; originally built by the French, it passed into British hands before being handed over to the United States, it now houses a fine museum and hosts regular re-enactment events.

TOP
Lundy's Lane battle site. Although the battlefield is now covered by the city of Niagara Falls, the cemetery and museum are well worth a visit. This view looks in the direction of Scott's advance; the area where the 21st US Infantry advanced is now a high school left of this viewpoint. (Author's collection)

BOTTOM
Fort Erie. In 1866 the ruins of the Old Fort were used as a base by Fenians (Irish Republicans) for their raid into Ontario, raids which hastened Confederation, and Canada became a nation in 1867. In 1937 reconstruction began as a make-work project, and the fort reopened on 1 July 1939. (Author's collection)

Since shortly after the war ended the attraction that the two waterfalls – American Falls and Horseshoe Falls – are best viewed from the Canadian side, has seen tourism develop as a major economic factor. Today the battlefield at Lundy's Lane has been effectively absorbed into the city of Niagara Falls, although the cemetery remains as an effective focal point – it contains a number of monuments and significant graves – and from it the importance of the high ground is readily apparent. Looking to the north of the highway, the slope up and down which the British launched their counterattacks is now covered by housing, as is most of the surrounding area, but the splendid little Lundy's Lane museum is just 70m away.

By contrast Chippawa is a fine preserved battlefield park, and looks much as it did at the time of the campaign. Although there is some encroachment by housing on the northern side of the battlefield, and a golf course also covers part of where the British approached and formed up, there is a wide expanse of the plain remaining, bounded on one side by the river and on the other side by woods, just as it was at the time of the battle, on which it gives an excellent perspective.

The main part of Fort Erie is also still in existence, surrounded by parkland, although the area of the British lines has been given over to housing. The fort itself was rebuilt in the late 1930s and is the scene of regular re-enactments, with the 'blowing of the bastion' being one of the highlights of the season. A number of archaeological digs have also been carried out in the area, most notably at Snake Hill, and these have yielded invaluable information about the lives of the soldiers that fought there. Between the main sites it is possible to follow the routes that the armies took and numerous notice boards have been placed to mark significant sites, and at Cook's Mills there stands a memorial cairn.

BIBLIOGRAPHY

The reader interested in learning more about the Niagara battles of 1814 can do no better than to start with the magisterial study by Donald E. Graves, *Where Right and Glory Lead!*, or his re-edited version of J. Mackay Hitsman's *The Incredible War of 1812*, both published by Robin Brass Studio of Montreal. Below is a select bibliography of sources covering the period.

Barbuto, Richard V., *Niagara, 1814: America Invades Canada* Lawrence, KA: University Press of Kansas, 2000 – excellent overview from the American perspective.

Berton, Pierre, *Flames Across the Border: The Canadian-American Tragedy, 1813–1814* Boston: Little, Brown, 1981 – a popular Canadian account.

Cruikshank, E. A. (ed.), *Documents Relating to the Invasion of the Niagara Peninsula by the United States Army, Commanded by General Jacob Brown, in July and August, 1814* Niagara-on-the-Lake, ON: The Niagara Historical Society, 1920

— *The Siege of Fort Erie, August 1st–September 23rd 1814* Welland, ON: Lundy's Lane Historical Society Publications, 1905

Fitz-Enz, David G., *The Final Invasion: Plattsburgh, the War of 1812's Most Decisive Battle* New York: Cooper Square Press, 2001 – A somewhat sensational account.

Graves, Donald E., (ed.), *Merry Hearts Make Light Days: The War of 1812 Journal of Lieutenant John Le Couteur, 104th Foot* Ottawa, ON: Carleton University Press, 1993

— *Red Coats & Grey Jackets: The Battle of Chippawa, 5 July 1814* Toronto, ON: Dundurn, 1994

— *Where Right and Glory! The Battle of Lundy's Lane, 1814* Toronto: Robin Brass Studio, 1997 – a truly masterful battle narrative.

— (ed.), *Soldiers of 1814: American Enlisted Men's Memoirs Of The Niagara Campaign by Jarvis Hanks, Amasiah Ford and Alexander McMullen* Youngstown, NY: Old Fort Niagara Association, 1995

— 'William Drummond and the Battle of Fort Erie', *Canadian Military History*, Vol. 1 (1992), 25–44

Hitsman, J. Mackay (ed. D. E. Graves), *The Incredible War of 1812: A Military History* Toronto, ON: Robin Brass Studio, 1999 – The most comprehensive Canadian account.

Johnson, Timothy D, *Winfield Scott: The Quest for Military Glory* Lawrence, KS: University Press of Kansas, 1998

Litt, Paul, Williamson, Ronald F. and Whitehorne, Joseph W. A., *Death at Snake Hill: Secrets from a War of 1812 Cemetery* Toronto, ON: Dundurn, 1993 – an archaeological study.

Lossing, Benson J., *The Pictorial Field-Book of the War of 1812* (Facsimile of the 1869 edition) Somersworth, NH: New Hampshire Publishing Company, 1976

Malcomson, Robert, *Lords of the Lake: The Naval War on Lake Ontario, 1812–1814* Toronto: Robin Brass Studio, 1998 – excellent study of the crucial naval rivalry on Lake Ontario.

Morris, John D., *Sword of the Border: Major General Jacob Jennings Brown, 1775–1828* Kent, OH: Kent State University Press, 2000

Skaggs, David C., *Thomas Macdonough: Master of Command in the Early U.S. Navy* Annapolis, MD: Naval Institute Press, 2003

Turner, Wesley B., *British Generals in the War of 1812: High Command in the Canadas* Montreal, QB and Kingston, ON: McGill-Queen's University Press, 1999

INDEX

References to illustrations are shown in **bold**. Plates are prefixed pl, with captions on the page in brackets.